THRESHOLD
OF
DISCOVERY

A FIELD GUIDE TO SPIRITUALITY IN MIDLIFE

L. ROGER OWENS

CHURCH
PUBLISHING
INCORPORATED

For
Simeon, Silas, and Mary Clare

Church Publishing
19 East 34th Street
New York, NY 10016
www.churchpublishing.org

Cover design by Paul Soupiset
Typeset by Denise Hoff

A record of this book is available from the Library of Congress.

ISBN-13: 978-1-64065-050-3 (pbk.)
ISBN-13: 978-1-64065-051-0 (ebook)

Printed in the United States of America

Contents

Introduction

I knew I was standing on the threshold of midlife.

You know it when you're there—the way you forget the name of an acquaintance you haven't seen in two months; the way you walk into the kitchen and forget what you came for—into the bedroom, into the bathroom, into the basement and forget why you're there; the way the white hairs on your head purchase more real estate each day; the way your sixth-grade son, who stands almost as tall as you, can rattle off names of apps you've never heard of like you used to be able to recite the starting lineup of the 1984 division-winning Chicago Cubs.

The way your friends from graduate school start getting divorced, or start getting cancer, and you start checking more frequently the spots on your stomach to see if the edges change, become uneven. The way you begin to fear you might lose this beautiful life you've been given—death, tragedy seem ever more possible—and *at the same time* you begin to fear that this beautiful life you've been given might actually be the one you're stuck with.

I knew I was on the threshold of midlife; my fortieth birthday was just two months away. It never occurred to me that it might also be a threshold of discovery. But that's exactly the phrase Sister Anna used, and I immediately warmed to it.

We were talking about my feet, at least I was—not the typical subject of conversation with a spiritual director. But it had not been a typical season in my life. Until recently my feet had never hurt. But that week, as my dad used to say, "My dogs were barking." None of my shoes were comfortable anymore. One Tuesday I stood teaching for two and a half hours and my arches and heels burned. I sat on the sofa in my office, pulled of my Gold Toe socks, massaged my feet, and hoped a student wouldn't walk in. I also made a plan, because I had to teach again that night.

I went hunting for new shoes before my evening class. I skipped all the places I usually shopped—any store in a strip mall; any store where I could see stacked shoe boxes and had to fetch my own; any store where the clerks knew little about shoes and less about feet; any store with the words "famous" or "show" in the name—and I drove straight to the shoe store recommended by a man thirty years older than I: Little's Shoes in the Squirrel Hill neighborhood of Pittsburgh, an old, family owned store just a few miles from where I teach.

A clerk greeted me at the door, and I offered a précis of my problem. He led me to the men's section and said he knew what I needed. He was surprisingly empathic. "I've been working here since high school twenty-five years ago," he said. "I think I can help you."

He brought out two styles in two different brands, laced a pair and put them on my feet. I walked, I skipped, I jumped a little. My dogs stopped barking. I happily spent twice as much as I've ever paid for dress shoes.

I wore those shoes in Sister Anna's office that day, but the story about my feet was a circuitous way to deeper issues. My newly aching feet accompanied other changes, shifts along the fault lines of my soul. As at sundown, when a familiar place begins to look strange, unfamiliar—that inviting shade tree now ominous in the twilight—so the lighting on the landscape of my spirit had been changing, imperceptibly at first, until it began to look like a place I'd never been before.

First, I noticed: words—how the old, religious words, faithful, trustworthy words, the words that comprised the hymns I loved to sing, the words I had said and explained and illustrated in so many sermons, words I wrote about in a theology dissertation—church, sin, incarnation, Trinity, atonement, resurrection, salvation, faith—these words began to leach their meaning. My confidence in them waned. I noticed it in my preaching and lecturing. I continued to utter them but felt inauthentic. And I noticed it as I listened to sermons—in the seminary chapel, in my home congregation. The language of my religion began to sound like the adults in *A Charlie Brown Christmas*.

When Sister Anna asked how I experienced God, I had no ready answer.

When she asked about my image of God, I had nothing to say.

My faith, it seemed, was being reduced, but I didn't know yet if it would end up like a red wine reduction sauce, reduced to its essence, its greatest intensity; or, like a boiling pot of water left on the stove, reduced to nothing at all.

I wondered aloud if I might be entering a dark night of the soul.

That's when Sister Anna spoke: "It sounds less to me like a dark night, and more like a threshold of discovery."

Threshold of discovery.

I remembered something psychiatrist and spiritual guide Gerald May had written: "When the spiritual life feels so uprooted, it can be almost impossible to believe—or even consider—that what's really going on is a graceful process of liberation—a letting go of old limiting habits, to make room for a fresh openness to love." In other words, a threshold of discovery.

That's the phrase that stuck with me, sticks with me still, the phrase that convinced me to stop imagining another life and consider the reality of this God-haunted one as I enter midlife's uprooting.

The one that eventually compelled me to buy a walking stick and take forty hikes.

The drama of turning forty is a cultural artifice—the "over-the-hill" birthday cards, "R.I.P." yard signs. Why not thirty-eight, or forty-two?

For my fortieth birthday party we invited a few families we knew from church for dinner and games. Only one family followed the cultural script. The box they gave me was large and taped together. When I opened it, I saw why it had to be so large—it had to fit a cane, silver with a big curved handle, nursing-home style. *Ah, the fortieth birthday gag gifts*: a bag of prunes, a package of sugar-free Werther's candies, an oversized pill box with the days of the week marked in enormous letters. Each gift said, "Now you are *old*." We all laughed, and my kids fought over the pill box.

Turning forty might be a time to laugh as a healthy response in a culture hypersensitive to age, but in Scripture the number forty has a more serious resonance.

The Israelites crossed a threshold, the Red Sea. Freedom was their possession, their new *modus operandi*. But they didn't know how to live freely; they could not remember their ancestors who had lived in freedom before a Pharaoh arose who knew not Joseph. Bondage had been their lot. They had their own discoveries to make. They had to discover their identity as a people: who they were without the Egyptians to tell them they were nothing but cheap labor. They also had to discover who this God was who freed them now that they did not have the violent lords of Egypt ruling them. Sometimes they felt it might be better to retrace their steps, preferring the certainties of bondage over the vagaries of freedom.

For forty years they practiced being a free people in this liminal space, this threshold. Many times they faltered. A whole generation died. At one point they decided it wasn't for them, that God couldn't be trusted, so they made for themselves another god and said, "*This* is the god who brought us out of Egypt!"

Since then, the number forty has signified the trials of transition, the ache of self-discovery, the turmoil of finding and abandoning comfortable images of God, of following a God you can never pin down. Forty years in the wilderness: a threshold of discovery minus the romance, minus the allure. Painful discovery.

I wonder if these forty years were on Jesus's mind when he, on the threshold of his short-lived mission in the world, was driven into the wilderness for forty days. The Israelites, through the Red Sea; Jesus, through baptism in the Jordan; both, into the wilderness after the water.

I can close my eyes and picture the scene of the Spirit descending on Jesus like a dove, but in my imagination the Spirit morphs into a screeching hawk and chases him into the wilderness where for forty days he followed the pattern established for God's people: he had to discover who he was and whether this God who called him by name and imbued his life with purpose was trustworthy, and whether he had it in him to trust. A voice from heaven told Jesus at his baptism, "You are my Son, the beloved, with you I am well pleased." Being told that is one thing; knowing it in the body's fleshy heart and the soul's mysterious depths—that's quite another.

That kind of knowing requires *forty*.

If it was true for God's people, true for Jesus, why shouldn't it be true for us? Why wouldn't we come to a threshold in our lives, like midlife, when the focus on establishing and proving ourselves changes, when the "dreams of fame and fortune," as Frederick Buechner calls them, are set to one side long enough for us to romp around in the reality of our lives and wrestle with the questions our four-decade pursuit of whatever we've been pursuing hasn't left room for?

As I approached this threshold I began to realize that I wanted to explore it, to step into this new territory with a degree of intentionality. These currents of change—of fear and hope and doubt and pain—I didn't want to ignore them or escape them. I wanted to explore. I didn't want the gentle Spirit to have to drive its talons into my shoulders and drag me across. I wanted to walk into forty and beyond slowly, with eyes wide open.

I had the idea on a walk at Beechwood Farms, an Audubon nature reserve three miles from our home.

During the summer we'd come here to pick up our weekly share of local farm produce. Dillner Farms, twenty miles north of where we live, designates the park as a pick-up spot, so we drove over each Tuesday, never sure what we were going to get, hoping for strawberries and not kohlrabi.

This time it was the day after Thanksgiving, unseasonably warm, and twenty days before my fortieth birthday. Other families like ours were seizing the opportunity to burn the calories from that second (in my case, third) piece of pumpkin pie and make space for leftovers that evening. After about an hour—after the kids had started complaining, pleading to *finally* go to the play area, and after the birds had taken their late morning break from singing and foraging—I had the thought: *I will take forty walks here in the year after I turn forty to mark this threshold-crossing into midlife.*

As I ruminated on this unbidden gift of an idea, it became a plan, something I needed to do. I would take these forty walks. I would observe the changes—the barren winter into the verdant spring, the spring into the lush summer, the summer into the polychromatic fall—and notice the changing seasons of my own soul at the same time—places of barrenness, places where the mind and soul felt stripped like the leaves of fall, places where a new faith or vocational yearnings were beginning to bud. Instead of trying to escape these changes of body and soul, like some do during a so-called midlife crisis, I would watch them, interrogate them, understand them. I would take these walks to make the discoveries that were still mine to make.

These walks, I thought, would become a chance for me to look in and up and down and around and ask God, "What are you up to in my life, and are you really where that famous breastplate of St. Patrick says you are, even though I don't always feel you there: before me, behind me, in the mouths of those who speak to me, in the eyes of those who see me? And what difference does it make, anyway?"

I would walk my way into midlife. But I would do it only three miles from home.

Others have done it differently, more adventurously. Elizabeth Gilbert ate, prayed, and loved her way around the world in her thirties. Bill Bryson walked the Appalachian Trail and gave us the gift of *A Walk in the Woods*. The biblical character known as the prodigal son—he had to have been about forty, right?—asked his father for his share of the inheritance and squandered it on riotous living, as the story goes.

But I've never been adventurous; most of my time spent walking in nature had been on a golf course until I sold my clubs a decade ago. And also, these adventures can feel like attempts to escape, or at least avoid. And some people might need that. Who hasn't felt the urge toward escape?

So I would escape about once a week, or so, into these meadows and woods, these hills and the valleys, so close they are practically in my backyard. I would never walk so far that I could forget I have commitments and responsibilities and obligations that comprise the fabric of my life; never so far that I could forget the joys and fears and anxieties that help make me who I am; never so far that I could forget these kids who don't say, "Bye," as I walk out the door because their noses are aimed at a screen and their ears are clogged by earbuds. Never so far that I wouldn't sometimes be able to bring them along, or bring my wife along, or invite a friend.

The prodigal son went into a far country and there discovered himself. I was going to stay closer to home.

Because I suspected that staying close would be key to discovering a spirituality for midlife. I wouldn't do it by going someplace new and bold, but by revisiting the familiar again and again, by staying in the backyard of my own life. After all, my life is the one thing I cannot escape. Even when I try, it always comes with me, this life. If I was going to cross this threshold well—and the crossing can take twenty years, they say—I suspected staying close to home might be key.

And this: if there was one thing I still believed with something close to the certainty of faith, it was that God is not somewhere else. So three miles away would be as good as three thousand.

One more reason: I could spare the expense of walking the Appalachian Trail or the Camino de Santiago, with all that expensive gear. I only needed one thing. I already had a pair of Rockports, grandfatherly-looking walking shoes I bought shortly after my new dress shoes, and a Tilley, a hat that matched my wife's, which we bought on our honeymoon thirteen years ago. But I didn't have a walking stick. If Moses needed a staff for his forty, so would I.

So two days after Christmas and two weeks after my fortieth birthday, I drove to the shop at the Audubon center. The walking sticks huddled in an umbrella stand just inside the door near the thirty-percent-off Christmas kitsch. I tried them all. I leaned on them, compared their weights and lengths, tested their textures against the palm of my hand. I put aside the one with the broken compass on the top, the arrow always pointing to the "S." I certainly hoped I wouldn't need the one with the animal-track identification guide tacked to it. If I ever needed to distinguish between a cougar print and a bear track, I would just go home.

The clerk sensed my growing decision paralysis. "I've always liked the hickory ones," he said—the very one I was holding. It was plenty tall, just the right length for me to put both hands on the top and rest my chin on my hands. It was the right staff to support me, to rest my weight against. To part Harts Run, perhaps, if it ever should exceed its banks.

You think about these things: what you need with you to walk into midlife with a changing faith and an aching body and an elusive God. And you acquire a staff, something to lean on. Maybe you also need insight, the stories of someone who has explored this territory—reflections and investigations that can be your companion as you make your way into the backyard of your own life at its midpoint and get to know it better, maybe for the first time. Surely many of your concerns will be the same, the slopes and the valleys to explore will be similar: the inevitability of death; slow, ineluctable change; questions about faith and identity and God; a shifting sense of vocation; the longing to make a difference; boredom and ennui; the bane and blessing of relationships. How we live into these themes, and how they differ from the way we experienced them in the first half of our lives— that's what makes up the spirituality of midlife.

That's what this book is about: these overarching themes, explored in one particular year and through the life of one particular forty-year-old who took forty walks to reflect on them and make his discoveries so that you can take this book with you as you step across your threshold or continue your own exploration. So that along with your walking stick—whatever or whoever that happens to be in your life—you will have these stories to lean on.

———

It's January 1, 2:50 in the afternoon. It's cold, Pittsburgh cold, even in an El Niño year. I'm wearing the thermal underwear I bought on sale at the mall last March, jeans, a long-sleeved t-shirt, and the winter jacket I picked up in October for five dollars at the Presbyterian Church harvest fair. I'm wearing a cap that makes me look like my grandfather, only mine has hidden earflaps that I can deploy to protect my ears from the wind chill. I'm wearing leather gloves. I'm holding my staff. I'm about to walk out.

Mary Clare, our six-year-old, is having a breakdown, a kindergarten hangover, unrecovered from a late New Year's Eve and too much sparkling grape juice. She's screaming, "I don't want you to go." But I'm going. As much as I hate to leave my wife, Ginger, with tired, whining kids, I announced yesterday my plan to take this walk. I kiss Mary Clare on the cheek and tell her I'll be back soon.

The door slams behind me, and the crying is muted by the seals of the exterior door and the winter wind rushing past my uncovered ears. I listen to the classical station on the short drive, winding down two curvy miles of Fairview Road, and I can feel myself relaxing. I am looking forward to this.

The first thing I see when I pull into the gravel drive is something I don't expect: other people. I didn't know about something called the First Day Hike. I didn't know that some American Hiking Society had given it a name and convinces thousands of people to walk tens of thousands of miles on New Year's Day each year. If I had known I might have waited until January 2, not wanting to be part of a fad.

But on January 1, I don't know this, so I wonder, *Are all of these people turning forty?*

— TRAIL ONE —

Facing Death and Change

I rebel against death, yet I know that
it is how I face death's inevitability
that is going to make me less or more fully alive.

–Madeleine L'Engle

Suppose we speak of the death of a cloud.
You look up in the sky and don't see
your beloved cloud anymore, and you cry,
"O my beloved cloud, you are no longer there.
How can I survive without you?" And you weep.

–Thich Nhat Hanh

WALK 1

I Tell You a Great Mystery

This gift-giving opened palm of a place, it didn't ask me what I wanted to receive on my first walk, what gift besides maids-a-milking I wished for on this Eighth Day of Christmas. If it had, I might have chosen a different image to notice, an alternate koan to contemplate, to circle in my mind as my feet stumble along this still unfamiliar terrain. Maybe I should have started in May, when nature's hands would have held out to me rainbows, bluebirds, butterflies, and other assorted wonders of spring.

But not on this day. Today it asks me to begin with the end in mind. It gives me a gift it will take some time to fully unwrap. On the other hand: Why not? Why not step into the threshold with this difficult mystery in mind?

As I park, I see two perky couples are getting out of an SUV. A double-date aura hangs about them, a flirtatious manner as they skip to the playground, radiating youthful energy. *No, they are not turning forty*, I think. *They are half my age.*

I consult my map and start along the same route my family took when we were here after Thanksgiving: past the shop and the education center on the left, to the entrance of the Upper Fields trail, which will lead me to the Spring Hollow trail. I notice the brown brush ranged along the path. Since there is no snow, I can see how leaves still cover the ground. The green grass on Upper Fields transitions to gravelly dirt as the trail inclines. A few red honeysuckle berries hang on an otherwise bare bush.

As the path turns upward, a mystery: at shoulder height to my right, a red length of yarn, a few inches long, dangles from a branch. Another one hangs fifteen yards ahead, and another after that. These did not grow here; someone tied them on purpose, and I can't imagine why.

Near the top of the first short incline, I pass beneath a dead tree that has snapped six feet from the ground and fallen above the path, lodging itself in the forked trunk of a tree on the other side, just high enough for me to walk under without ducking. The splinters, rough and sharp at the break, rise like stalagmites from the trunk where the gray-brown bark has fallen off, exposing the pale wood.

As I inspect the tree my field of vision widens, and I see what I have not registered until now—signs of death all around me: dozens more like this toppled tree, fallen this way and that like the dead on a battlefield; barren ground beneath my feet; brown leaves, cloaking the frozen earth like a pall; denuded trees, vulnerable, exposed; the deep silence of winter. All of it contrasts sharply with the *joie de vivre* of the couples I saw when I arrived, as if to say, *It all comes to an end. It doesn't last, not the energy of youth, not life itself.* The varied and vivid shades of life fade into the mundane tones of death. It can come with a sudden, brittle break, as with the tree, or with the slow loss of chlorophyll in the leaves. And what part of creation is immune to this process?

"The heavens tell the glory of God and the earth declares God's handiwork," says Psalm 8. But today creation seems to be declaring something else, what another psalm affirms: "As for mortals, their days are like grass; they flourish like a flower in the field; for the wind passes over it, and it is gone, and its place knows it no more."

As I continue, I can't shake the image of the tree or the lesson of the psalm. I wonder if I am uncovering the gift I am to receive on my first walk. Is the beginning of midlife too soon to ponder these things—death and decay in general, and also the inevitability of my own?

"Thanks," I mutter under my breath, not sure if I mean it. Maybe those maids-a-milking would have been better. But I realize I am primed to see these things, more ready than I might have expected.

A few days ago Ginger and I lingered at the dinner table while the kids played in the family room. Usually we all leave the table at the same time, the kids to take their plates to the kitchen, Ginger to put away leftovers, and I to my dishwashing post. But not that night.

"I can't believe she's dead," Ginger said, almost inaudibly. "And I can't imagine what Susan's going through."

Ginger grew up with Susan. They went to high school together, served on youth mission trips together, sang in the same choirs. Ginger had just learned that Susan's twelve-year-old daughter had died of leukemia.

Ginger said she couldn't imagine, but, of course, we could imagine: the clothes in the laundry basket that would never be worn again; the laundry basket that would sit there for months until a gentle friend or relative convinced her it was time; the unmade bed; the way the grocery bill would be a little less each month, and there would be no need to remember to buy Captain Crunch, a favorite cereal; the way she would avoid the cereal aisle altogether. We *could* imagine, and that's what broke our hearts. We sat silently, listening to the giggles of our children and aching for a mother who would hear giggles now only in her memory.

Yes, I have been prepared to notice these things.

For the past couple of months two students have been coming to my office every other week for their independent study. We have been studying the themes of grief and lament in Christian memoir. Along with books that have become classics, like *A Grief Observed* by C.S. Lewis and *Lament for a Son* by Nicholas Wolterstorff, we read Madeleine L'Engle's memoir, *Two-Part Invention*, that weaves the story of her meeting her husband, Hugh, with the last months of his life as he succumbed to cancer. I also required the students to read novelist Ann Hood's memoir *Comfort*, the account of her and her family's grief after her five-year-old daughter died suddenly from a virulent form of strep.

"If this book does not make you weep," I warned my students, "I'll wonder if you're human."

Hood's is not a Christian memoir, but I wanted my students, who are preparing to be pastors, to see how she describes her and her husband's visits with pastors and rabbis as they sought comfort in their grief. "Foolishly, I believed that clergypeople might hold the answers I screamed to God for every night. . . . But I saw how their eyes drifted toward the clocks on their walls, and when an hour had passed, they assured us time would heal and sent us on our miserable way." I wanted my students to hear her words, to feel her indictment of our work.

And to appreciate her discovery. Three years after her daughter's death, she writes, "Our loss still filled our home, every corner of it. It still filled us. Time doesn't heal, I had learned, it just keeps moving. And it takes us with it."

And now, I wonder, is she alluding to that hymn, the one I know we'll sing on the first Sunday of the New Year, the truth of which even a middle-aged doubter can't question, however much he might want to avoid it?

> *Time, like an ever rolling stream, bears all who breathe away;*
> *They fly forgotten, as a dream, dies at the opening day.*

The prayer request in worship the Sunday before Christmas also made me think of this hymn. "Pray for the family of Frank Thompson," Laura said, and I saw a few nods of recognition as she filled in the details. Frank was coaching his daughter's basketball practice when he collapsed on the court and died instantly of a heart attack, with his daughter watching; Frank was forty-two.

Time doesn't heal. It just keeps moving. And it takes us with it.

The invitation to consider the inevitable is all around us, but we have so much else to think about that we push these thoughts away, repress them as thoroughly as we can.

Until a walk in the woods opens your eyes to what you've been hiding from, been defended against for decades. Until a snapped-off tree invites you to face the fact of mortality.

Upper Fields meets Spring Hollow a hundred yards beyond the fallen tree. Spring Hollow slopes into a valley after it passes between two stately chestnut oaks a yard apart, sentries guarding the entrance to the valley below. A rapid descent with three switchback curves, and I'm in the valley heading back in the direction of the parking lot.

Eventually I arrive at Harts Run. This still-trickling stream testifies to the above-average temperatures of this winter. I hear the water sluicing beneath the footbridge, rolling under me and down into the valley toward the road that takes its name from this trickle: Harts Run Road.

Living water—that's what some streams of Christianity would call this, those that insist baptisms be performed in flowing water. No dunk tank or swimming pool or still-as-ice lake, but rippling, living water. There's not enough water here to submerge a new convert, though plenty for a Methodist, Presbyterian, or Episcopal sprinkling. Watching it, I recall that Jesus told a woman at a well that living water would spring forth from her soul. Here is a source of life for birds, squirrels, chipmunks—who knows what else. For the deer that pant for flowing streams just like this one.

My prayer book has the minister say at some point in a funeral, "In the midst of life, we are in death," as if those gathered need the reminder. And that seems to be the lesson being impressed on me as I stand here above the stream: in the midst of life, indeed, we are in death, *so stop avoiding it.* After all, I have just walked through a valley of death—the fallen trees, like a community of dead comrades; the not-yet-decomposed leaves; the gray winter sky blanketing me like a shroud. But when the clouds break briefly and I see the flashing of daylight in the stream's mini-waves, it occurs to me the opposite is true as well: in the midst of death, we are in life.

Spring Hollow leads me out of the valley. A few sharp turns, some panting as I climb, and I'm back on level ground. The path widens and straightens, and at the end, though I can't see it yet, is the play area to which the perky couples bounded, flaunting their youthfulness.

As I walk in that direction, behold!, a snippet of red yarn tied to a twig. But not yarn alone this time; from the yarn dangles a pine cone. *Of course—mystery solved.* In my mind I can see a kindergarten class here on a field trip, twenty bundles of energy huddled around tables in the activity room, gluing bits of yarn onto pine cones, then messily dabbing peanut butter onto each scale, and pressing birdseed into the peanut butter: kid-made birdfeeders.

"You are helping the birds survive the winter," I imagine the activity director saying, "because it's hard for them to find food when it's snowy." These kids are agents of life, kids for whom it's too soon to contemplate the braided mystery:

> *In the midst of life, we are in death.*
> *In the midst of death, we are in life.*

But at forty, it's not too soon for me.

Some mysteries are easier to solve than others. And some mysteries are not meant to be solved but inhabited. "Behold, I tell you a great mystery," the apostle Paul wrote as he tried to make sense of the sting of death and the power of resurrection. I wonder, as I walk past the pavilion by the pond, now able to see the playground and the parking lot just past it, if the simple Christian narrative many of us have adopted—life, death, heaven, with its confident assurance of the immortality of the soul—shields us from what seems to be the necessary task of exploring this mystery: death in life, life in death, woven inseparably together, the two, part of God's story, part of the story of this place, part of creation's story from very close to the beginning.

And, I'm beginning to see, part of my story as well.

WALK 2

The Word God Might Whisper

Today you wouldn't know it's winter. Silas, our ten-year-old, still wears his hoodie, but Simeon, our twelve-year-old, has tied his sweatshirt around his waist. We trek across ground muddy from a recent thaw that followed the five inches of snow we received a week ago. Sixty-five degrees and sunny: I'm glad for this reprieve. I feel hopeful—*Could this weather last?*—hopeful and out of breath.

"Slow down. Let me catch up," I say. I never expected to need my walking stick so soon, but today I do.

When people ask me how I'm doing, they often say, "Well, you had the laparoscopic kind, right? That's supposed to be a lot easier." Sure, this heals quicker than a six-inch incision, but today, two weeks later, I'm still weak and sore.

But I'm alive, which is not, I admit, a complete surprise, even though the risk of death under general anesthesia is on the rise—seven deaths per million, as of a few years ago. But anytime you sign the form acknowledging the risk, and your wife stands in the doorframe and cries as they wheel you into the operating room, it's a more concrete opportunity to reflect on death than most Friday mornings provide.

On Thursday, January 14, I stood from a chair in a small room in the church basement, having finished leading the first week of a twelve-week study on spiritual disciplines. We ended with a poem by Denise Levertov, "The Avowal," considering its images of resting in God. She invites the reader, like a swimmer, to dare to float on their back, invites the reader to imagine floating in God, and I invited those present to dare such trust.

As I stood, I felt a dull ache in my back where my lower ribs attach to my vertebrae. I blamed the chair, old and hard, suspected that sitting in it for an hour had triggered arthritis pain, which I've been used to for years. As I drove home, the pain intensified and spread, sharpened. By the end of the eight-minute drive the pain radiated to the front of my ribs, sternum, and right shoulder. An hour later, pain was swallowing my whole torso, and Ginger was driving me to the emergency room.

Mention "chest" and "pain" together at the reception desk in the ER and they waste no time. A nurse whisked me to a room and began an EKG. Then blood tests, an x-ray, a CAT scan, by which time a second dose of morphine had given me minimal relief, allowing me to lie still for the scan. "When I inject the contrast dye, you're going to feel like you're wetting yourself," the technician said helpfully. "Don't worry, you're not."

Back in the room, a physician announced good news and bad: I wasn't having a heart attack, but my gallbladder was horribly inflamed. She ordered a stronger narcotic, Dilaudid, and scheduled surgery for the next day.

My post-Dilaudid memory is hazy, but I remember two things that mattered.

By eight in the morning they were ready to wheel me to the OR antechamber. I said goodbye to the children, who looked more unsure than they had the night before. Ginger said she would run them to school and return before the surgery and told me Pastor Tom was on the way.

In the corridor, as the orderly pushed my bed toward the prep room, I experienced an urge to confess. Surely, before surgery, before a general anesthesia from which there's the slightest chance you might not awaken, my conscience began to suggest, surely it's wise to offer a confession, and I felt the need to ask forgiveness for a host of things: for my angry impatience with my children; for not being as attentive a husband as I should be; for ripping up that picture of Sarah Conder, my older brother's crush in sixth grade, and then denying it; for leaving *reading knowledge of Latin, Greek, Hebrew, German, and French* on my CV because I had passed reading comprehension exams in those languages, though I had failed to maintain what little facility I once had. And for my more recent faintness of faith, my intermittent wondering if the God to whom I needed to confess was even real.

I suffered a sudden case of scrupulosity, and I felt afraid, and sorry for the unsuspecting orderly on whom I was about to unload my guilt. Then I remembered the previous day's Eucharist service in chapel at the seminary where I teach. I was the celebrant, the one with the privilege of reading and preaching the Scriptures, of leading those gathered in prayer, and of inviting them to the table where I would do my best to point them to Jesus, the host of the sacred feast.

Before inviting them to the table, I led a corporate prayer of confession. And then, as the ordained clergy person, I looked around the circle of worshipers—students of mine, friends and colleagues, administrators (who happened miraculously to be also friends and colleagues)—and I said, "In the name of Jesus Christ, you are forgiven." Then they said to me—all thirty of them in one voice the church calls the voice of Christ's body—what their baptisms had commissioned them to say: "In the name of Jesus Christ, you are forgiven."

This cloud of witnesses suddenly surrounded me while I was lying on my back, smoothly gliding through a nondescript hospital corridor, and spoke to me in my imagination, reminded me that one of the last things anyone had done for me was to announce that my slate had been wiped clean, polished even for extra luster. I don't know if the orderly could tell, but at that moment I believe the bed got easier to push, got a little lighter.

That was the first thing I remember that mattered.

A few minutes later my pastor walked into the prep room. I was surprised how glad I was to see him. He asked if he could read a psalm and pray for me. I knew which psalm I wanted, but my drug-fogged mind couldn't summon the number—the list of drugs I'd been given by this time looked to me like the signatures on the Declaration of Independence. So Tom suggested Psalm 91, the very one I was struggling to recall. As he read this psalm of assurance, a declaration of God's protection—*For he will deliver you from the snare of the fowler and from the deadly pestilence; he will cover you with his pinions, and under his wings you will find refuge . . . you will not fear the terror of the night, or the arrow that flies by day, or the pestilence that stalks in the darkness, or the destruction that wastes at noonday*—tears began to stream down my cheeks.

When he finished, I looked at him through a saltwater blur, and I said the truest thing I could think to say, though not in the most eloquent of terms. "I really believe this stuff," I said—not a confession that will ever rank with Peter's "You are the Christ" or doubting Thomas's "My Lord and my God!" but it was good enough for Tom to use later in a sermon, appropriately cloaking my identity.

I'm not sure I knew what I meant. It was just a nod from deep within me, a sense of trust. It wasn't that I believed no harm would come to me. I knew better than that, knew that his praying a psalm over me was not an incantation, a spell to secure my safety. A prayer wouldn't magically keep me from becoming a statistic; some people had to be those seven per million. But I believed somehow, trusted at a fundamental level, that I was safe, that I had nothing to fear, that I would be OK, whatever that meant.

That was the second thing that I remembered, a little gift the older writers on spirituality would have called a consolation.

Ginger returned from taking the kids to school. Dr. Edwards, the surgeon, came to remind me of some of the risks of the surgery and get me—or was it Ginger?—to sign more papers. Dr. Go, the resident who would be assisting, cheerily introduced herself. Dr. Pickle, the anesthesiologist, said not-so-comfortingly to Ginger, "I can't stand here and say to you that there's not some chance of life-threatening complications from the anesthesia." She looked stricken with worry as they pushed me into the operating room.

Next thing I remember, the nurse anesthetist was pressing a plastic mask over my nose and mouth, telling me to breathe normally, that in just a few seconds I would be asleep.

"Aren't I supposed to count backwards from ten?"

"You can if you want to," she said.

"Well, that's what they do on TV and in the movies, count backwards from ten. Shouldn't I?"

"You can if you . . ."

Close curtain.

Anyone one who knows anything about Julian of Norwich, the fourteenth-century English mystic and saint, knows at least two things: She said, "All shall be well," and she saw a vision of a hazelnut. There are other things worth knowing about her—that she was a profound theologian, that she saw God as mother, that she was the first woman to write a book in English.

But it's Julian's hazelnut I think of now as Simeon runs up ahead with his brother, and I notice these few acorns missed by the squirrels during their fall gathering. The hazelnut's size amazed Julian. It represented all that God had made, all that is, including her, and yet: so small! Still God loves it, upholds it in being. Whatever happens, God claims the hazelnut and always will.

In one of my first meetings with Sister Anna a few months ago, I was struggling to express a sense of faith in the midst of doubt. She asked me a question, hoping to elicit some words that would express my deepest beliefs at the moment, and I felt ridiculous, because only one word came to me with conviction: *yes.* I didn't want to say it, it felt so silly. *You're a theologian who's published a seventy-thousand-word dissertation, and this is all you can come up with?*

I sat in silence on a small plaid sofa, a tiny lamp glowing faintly next to me, and Sister Anna waited, just a few feet away in her plush reading chair. I told her what I believed, in that moment: yes. Beneath the confusion, pain, and suffering in the world, beneath my own perplexity, anxiety, and doubt, stands the foundation of a divine *yes*, the affirmation that what is—including me—is created, loved, and upheld, and nothing can change that. As Julian's God told her, "I am keeping you very safe."

I'm glad to be alive, to walk through these woods with my boys on this last day of January, with a little help from a hickory walking stick. I'm glad this little corner of the hazelnut is close enough for me to explore, and that Ginger and these kids share this hazelnut with me. Yes, I say to all this. *Yes.*

But I also know, in a way I didn't just weeks before, and at a level that surprises me, that for forty years I have tried to secure my place on the hazelnut and make it permanent and impressive—a futile task. Someday I will not wake up after the final curtain—no more encores, not here at least. But if I do awaken somehow in God, I won't expect to see a bright light, and I don't know if I will see loved ones or recognize them, but I wonder if I might hear a word, just one.

Might God be willing to whisper to me, as God does to us all every second of our lives, if Julian is right: "Yes"?

Facing Change with Buddhism and St. Francis

I gave him the benefit of the doubt. When you're in fifth grade and your knowledge is expanding every day, you might quiz your parents because you're excited about the new thing you know, not to expose their ignorance.

Like many evenings, two nights ago we were gathered in the family room after Mary Clare had gone to bed. The boys loafed on the couch reading, their feet propped against the coffee table heaped with overdue library books, school papers, and cooking magazines. Ginger sat in the sea-mist chair we inherited from my grandmother. I sat swallowed by the new oversized La-Z-Boy. As I sink into it each night, I fear I might never get up.

Silas was reading a Civil War novel for literacy. He'd already tagged it with a fifth grader's go-to judgment: boring. But it must have reminded him of something he learned in class, because he looked up at us and asked, "What Civil War battle in April, 1862, was the bloodiest battle so far in American history?" The question underlined my thinking about change lately.

Change catalyzed this midlife experiment, and January's meditations on death led back here to death's fraternal twin: impermanence. In the first four decades of life, change, if we notice it at all or give it any thought, is nearly synonymous with progress. In the previous two decades of my own life change has meant graduating a couple times with ever more letters to put after my name, getting married and having three children, pastoring churches, and moving to places where I would earn more money. By almost any measure you'd count these changes as advances. *Forward ho*!

And then Silas innocently posed a question.

His asking highlighted the new reality of change: after forty, change, that devilish shapeshifter, disguises itself ever more frequently as decline.

Ginger and I glanced at each other, at a loss. I'm sure we had once aced exams on the Civil War. We knew the generals and the battles, the dates and the body counts. But the neural pathways in our brains now displayed "road closed" signs, and we couldn't reach the information.

I said the only name of a Civil War battle I could recall at the moment. "Gettysburg?"

"No, Shiloh."

Shiloh. Isn't that the name of a dog in a famous children's book? Or a town in the Bible where something significant happened? But the only Shiloh I could recall was the restaurant perched on Mt. Washington, which overlooks downtown Pittsburgh, where they serve gourmet macaroni-and-cheese, to which they will add anything you want—"As long as we have it in the kitchen," a waiter once quipped. On our last visit I ate lobster jalapeno mac-n-cheese topped with an over-easy fried egg. I won't soon forget that meal. But a Civil War battle?

"Ah, yes," I said, "Shiloh."

Today I reverse the route I took last month, and it doesn't take me long to realize I don't know where I'm going; everything looks different. I know I usually come out near the playground, so I head in that direction, a meadow of Canada thistle on my left, and beyond that, the pond, drained for the winter.

Once I'm on the path, the wind picks up. I pause next to the pond and the pavilion and look up, resting my hands and chin on my staff. Gray clouds crowd the sky, but a patch of blue hurries past as if late for an appointment, and then, as quickly as it appeared, it vanishes, swallowed up in the throng of gray.

I think of Mary Clare, how she and I like to watch the clouds as we sit on the sidelines of Silas's soccer games. I remember one crisp morning last fall, Mary Clare sitting next to me in a camp chair, wrapped in a pink fleece blanket. It's always colder out there than the kids expect—they never anticipate the wind—so we bring extra blankets, knowing they'll plead for warmth. That morning my burrito-wrapped daughter looked into the sky and spied something. "Look, Daddy. That cloud looks like a dog."

"Where?"

She pointed, but by the time I caught what she was pointing at, the dog had become, quite obviously to me, a hippopotamus. Over the next twenty minutes the score of the soccer game remained the same—as soccer scores are wont to do—but a whole zoo of animals floated by, many of them morphing right before our eyes. A flamingo, she swears, transformed into a princess castle. I thought it had become a BMW.

Why can't all change be so benign?

The sky is all gray again, and I am cold standing, so I move on.

From the time of Socrates to today, we humans have been biased against change. We prefer the stable, the perdurable. Everything changes, yes, no one can deny it, so we have placed on the transcendent our need for stability—Plato's forms, theology's impassible God—and then prefer earthly things that mimic the permanent, prove lasting: virtue, character, principle, mediocre Duke football—things we can count on to be, more likely than not, the same tomorrow as today.

But at the beginning of midlife, I can no longer avoid change, and must not. And the enduring religious traditions teach us to accept impermanence. That's why I've brought along a small book by Zen master Thich Nhat Hanh, because aren't Buddhists the experts at enlightening us on ways of living with impermanence and accepting the inevitability of death without being crushed by that awareness?

I had planned to read some here, but like my kids before a soccer game, I've underestimated the chilliness of the wind. I hurry through the final half-mile, up and out of the valley, and down the Upper Fields path toward the shop, education center, and parking lot. By the time I reach the car the sun has prevailed; the crowd of gray clouds has largely dispersed, and those lingering have exchanged their gray robes for white.

But it's too late for me. I'm going to the library to read my book.

———————

"Everything is impermanent; everything changes," Thich Nhat Hanh writes, and you won't find me arguing with him. But believing this truth doesn't help me deal with it. I can still resist.

To come to terms with change—to stop living in an illusory world of permanence, a world in which we gather, accumulate, and protect what we deem valuable, falsely believing we can secure our treasures and our lives, an imaginary world that drives greed and violence—Thich Nhat Hanh says to meditate on Buddhism's Five Remembrances, to let them sink into us, to get used to them so that we might lower our defenses against change, and live in something closer to reality. I'm willing to give it a try. Three of the five remembrances strike me immediately:

> I am of the nature to grow old. I cannot escape growing old.
> I am of the nature to die. I cannot escape death.
> All that is dear to me, and everyone I love, are of the nature to change.
> There is no way to escape being separated from them.

As I read, I feel myself assenting, and at the same time rebelling—and it's this rebellion I want to release. For how can I live the next decades of my life if I acknowledge this truth with my mind but fight it in my living?

"What we cherish, what belongs to us today, won't be there tomorrow; we will have to take leave, not only of our most cherished objects, but also of the people we love," Hanh writes. Is this the truth I'm going to need to contemplate, become comfortable with, to live well life's second half?

I've had to take leave of a father sooner than I would have liked, which was hard to accept. I struggle just as much when I consider what I cherish now. As I do, staring blankly at the shelves here in the back corner of the library, my throat catches. Not just my memory, or what's left of it, not just my mind and my vocation—yes, I cherish these things—but especially the ones who live with me and fill my life with joy and challenge, these people whose connection to me constitutes my life, these dear ones with their unique passions, quirks, and irreplaceable peculiarities.

Irreplaceable—heavens, yes. Permanent—dammit, no.

But I've learned enough from Hanh over the years to know what to do with this rising resistance. So I get as comfortable as I can in the wooden, straight-backed chair, and inhale slowly through my nose, saying to myself, "Breathing in, I feel my resistance to change," and then I exhale slowly, saying, "Breathing out, I release my resistance to change." After ten minutes of this, I'm ready to leave. I wonder what I'll be ready for after ten years of this, because that's what it will take, or longer.

I have this in my tradition too, I think as I exit the library.

"We will not fear, though the earth should change," the psalm says, and I realize I could have brought the Book of Psalms with me just as well. Or Ecclesiastes—the book of the wise one who teaches us it's vanity to work to secure a life, to bungee-cord your life together. You are born, you live, you die. Others are born to replace you; they live, they die; so it goes.

We have our own remembrance too, couched in Latin and out of fashion, what they called in the Middle Ages *memento mori*, the remembrance of death, an aspect of what writer Jon Sweeney calls the medieval "macabre fascination" with death. Death was inescapable, ubiquitous, after all, with no way to keep it out of sight as we do today. Think: plague, war, famine, disease; up close, next door, unmediated. And remembering death—keeping its frightening visage always in mind—helped people to straighten up and fly right, as the song goes. Death can come any time, and after that—judgment. And it's a fearful thing to fall into the hands of an angry God, or so they thought. *Memento mori*—motivation to live well.

But reading Sweeney's book reminded me that this approach to death wasn't the only one in the Middle Ages. There was the way of St. Francis, an outlier, acquainted with change and decline. In the waning years of his life his eyesight diminished, his body weakened, and the brothers began to squabble about the growing movement of the Franciscans. And Francis managed, in the midst of it all—in the midst of a culture that said, "Be afraid, be very afraid"—to befriend death, to welcome her as a sister. He somehow learned *not* to be afraid.

I want to overcome the fear of death, though I'm not ready for us to be friends, to share a Coke and a conversation. There's still too much beauty to enjoy, too many people to love, too many seasons of life to live. But I appreciate what makes Francis's welcoming of sister death possible, and different from Hanh's freedom from the fear of death: Francis trusted a divine steadfastness at the heart of the flux we call this world. Francis wasn't a metaphysician or a philosopher. He hadn't worked out a theory of the relationship between the Eternal and the temporal, but he knew the reason that psalm said we should not fear change—fire, flood, earthquake, death: God is our refuge and strength. And so Francis prayed, "Blessed be the Lord my God, for you have helped me, you were my stronghold when I was in trouble. To you, my defender, will I sing: My citadel is God himself, the God who loves me."

As his circumstances changed—as his eyesight weakened, as his fledgling order began to flail, as his own life ebbed away—he trusted that he was safe, that his identity was rooted and secure in another identity whose name is Love.

Now I know what I want to companion my growing acceptance of change, marked by these new gray hairs in my goatee that portend greater changes in years to come, even my eventual and final decline. Yes, I want the equanimity of Thich Nhat Hanh, but that's not all. I want a consoling trust to accompany me, what Christians have always called faith. The faith that, though what and whom I cherish will take leave of me, though I will one day take my final leave of this existence I have called life for forty years and hope to for many more, there is a Love that will not take leave of us, a Love that binds us to itself and to one another in unimaginable ways.

That when I leave this life, I will not have left the embrace of the Love that has held me thus far, through all my changes. That none of us will.

— TRAIL TWO —

Asking, "Who Am I Now?"

There are aspects of detachment and refinements of interior purity and delicacy of conscience that even the majority of sincerely holy men never succeed in discovering.

–Thomas Merton

For me to be a saint means to be myself.

–Thomas Merton

WALK 4

Swift Iron of Attachments

When it's early March in Pittsburgh and a rare sixty degrees, and the sun has emerged from its annual hibernation, here's what you do: You take your wife's suggestion and scrap the Asian beef dinner plan, you assemble lunchmeat sandwiches on Hawaiian bread rolls, wash some strawberries (recent arrivals from California), you fill a Tupperware with sugar-snap peas and baby carrots, you grab what's left of the tube of cheddar Pringles, and you take the whole family with you on your walk.

The kids go eagerly, especially Mary Clare. She brings along a clipboard, paper, and a green pen like mine so she can record what we see. (As it happens, on this walk we see chickadees, a cardinal, a dead vole, and a terrifyingly top-heavy turkey run downhill, take flight, and soar over a valley, which reminds me how I recently heard a paleontologist say that birds are dinosaurs, adding, "A turkey is basically a velociraptor.")

We head first to the pavilion by the pond to eat, and fight over the shards of Pringles huddled at the bottom of the tube. We discuss what we should plant in our garden this spring, arriving at near consensus: tomatoes and watermelons.

But we can't sit for long. Our intrepid six-year-old is ready to move. She takes the lead, and we follow her down the Spring Hollow trail in the same direction I went last time, into the valley, over Harts Run—she doesn't pause to let me appreciate its trickle—and soon to an area I don't immediately recognize. The landscape looks different each time I'm here, so we press on until I realize we should be able to see the tree-top lookout from this spot in the valley, but can't. The path is narrowing more than I remember, and it's guiding us into a pine stand that I've *never* seen before. By the time we're slipping on pine needles, I know we are on a trail less trodden, at least by me. The beginning of Thomas Merton's famous prayer comes to mind: "My Lord God, I have no idea where I am going." But Merton was praying about the search for his true self in God; for me, the question is less existential, more pedestrian: *Where are we?*

Somewhat familiar with the map, I make an informed guess. We are on a trail called Woodland, which will wind upward and reconnect with Spring Hollow or Upper Fields, detouring us about a half-mile—though I don't mention this to the boys, who are already advocating an about-face.

"We've learned our lesson," one of them mutters. "Never let the six-year-old lead."

I make an executive decision: we will keep going.

Ten minutes later, as the boys are nearing revolt-levels of frustration, Mary Clare shouts, "What's that?" She runs to an arrow planted in the ground a few yards off the path and yanks on it—harder than you'd think necessary to pull it free. A clump of mud rises with it, and we see why: three barbs on the tip of the arrow fan out when it hits its target, anchoring it in the flesh of whatever it strikes—in this case, earth.

"Can we keep it, please?" Unacquainted as we are with hunting and its deadly instruments, the arrow proves a fascinating find for our family. Mary Clare has completely forgotten the dead vole.

My mind travels back to Mr. Davis's twelfth-grade Latin class, to Dido in Virgil's *Aeneid*—Dido, the once regal and reasonable queen of Carthage, no longer herself, inflamed with love for Aeneas; Dido, a victim of goddess Juno's ploy to keep Aeneas from founding Rome, symbolized by a deer struck with an arrow. The *volatile ferrum*, the "swift iron," the arrow of passion—it stays in her: the "lethal arrow sticks in her side." *Infelix Dido*, unlucky Dido, Virgil calls her, in what seems to me an understatement.

I inspect the swift iron my daughter clutches and its villainous-looking barbs. *Lucky deer*, I think, *to have escaped this one.*

"No, we'll leave this treasure for other pirates to claim."

Thomas Merton wrote, "I wonder if there are twenty men alive in the world now who see things as they really are. That would mean that there were twenty men who were free, who were not dominated or even influenced by any attachment to any created thing or to their own selves or to any gift of God .... They are the ones who are holding everything together and keeping the universe from falling apart."

If I said right now I wanted to be free enough to join the elite club Merton claims is keeping the universe from falling apart, I would be overshooting a little. That's too much pressure. But I do want to see things as they really are, to see myself as I really am.

Merton teaches again and again that attachments—whatever we love for their own sakes, outside of their place in the horizon of God's creative embrace—blind us to reality and to our truest identities in God. Anything can become an attachment: a car, a friend, a job; images of ourselves, memories and fears, even our experiences of God. These things can land in us like arrows and make us forget ourselves.

I remember having an arrow-attachment pointed out to me. The summer before my family moved from North Carolina to Pittsburgh, I attended a final retreat with some clergy friends who had been meeting together for a few years. We invited Sister Joanna to lead an Enneagram workshop to help us gain deeper self-understanding. I don't remember what number I am on the Enneagram—five, maybe?— but I do remember the vice Sister Joanna said bedevils people with my number, because I erupted in guffaws of incredulity: avarice.

"Impossible!" I scoffed. "Ask anyone who knows me—I want to get rid of things. I don't accumulate. Greed, bah! I'm even trying to help our wedding china exit the house."

"But Roger," Sister Joanna said, "it doesn't have to be material things. Is there nothing you are greedy for—knowledge, perhaps, or recognition?" *Who invited her, anyway?*

A week later the truth of her words struck me. I stood in my study on the third floor of our parsonage, packing my books and wondering if I could lighten our load by giving some of them away. I love being surrounding by my books, the walls wrapped in shelves and sturdy book-spines staring at me from all directions. As I took each book and flipped through the pages, I fought a holy war in my soul over whether I could part with it.

That's when I saw it. These objects had become symbols of what I was greedy for, what I thought made me somebody, made me matter—my knowledge and expertise. They were reinforcing an image of myself I had been more than happy to wear as a mask.

How many more arrows, accumulated through forty years of living, are there for me to find? Do I careen through the city of my life like unlucky Dido, in a frenzy? Do I look like a scarecrow in a field used for hunting practice? Or like Sebastian, the third-century saint and martyr, usually depicted fastened to a post and pierced— as in one medieval painting—with fourteen arrows (though, as the story goes, these did not kill him—he was fetched and healed by Irene of Rome—so his persecutors clubbed him to death)?

What could be more necessary in these years when we feel the pull to discover our truest selves—the pull to turn our lives outward in love, to know the divine beyond the phrases we learned in catechism classes or Sunday school rooms, to lose ourselves in the Love that moves the earth and stars, to see ourselves and our world clearly, as they really are—what could be more necessary than to identify the wounding arrows of attachment and begin to heal?

No, I don't need to keep the universe from falling apart. It's hard enough to get my kids' lunches made every day. But I would like to know myself more honestly, and my attachments are like cataracts: they cloud my vision.

And it's just conceivable that my sight of God has blurred recently not only because God, in the mystery of transcendence, lies beyond the capacities of my mind, but that my unknowing attention to the arrows of attachment embedded in my heart has stolen my gaze from the God who, if Jesus is any reliable indication, really does long to be known—and longs for us to know ourselves.

We are not lost anymore. Woodland trail has deposited us onto Upper Fields, and we find our bearings. The gentle downhill from here relieves the boys. I'm now thinking about the rest of that Merton prayer. No longer physically lost, I can appreciate how it's the perfect prayer for these years called midlife, these years when we feel most acutely, perhaps, that we don't know where we're going. "My Lord God, I have no idea where I am going. I do not see the road ahead of me. I cannot know for certain where it will end. Nor do I really know myself."

Nor do I really know myself.

There are more masks to take off. More arrows to free from my soul. More wounds to expose to the healing air and light and Spirit. Which means, no doubt, more suffering.

"I will not fear," that prayer ends, "for you are ever with me, and you will never leave me to face my perils alone."

Even the peril of pulling out the barbs? I can only hope.

Inhabiting "But . . . Unlike"

Ginger joins me today. We're still enjoying this spring-like March near the end of our third winter in Pittsburgh. The first two were brutal. I grew up in Indiana, and I thought I knew something about winters. I thought I could tap into my childhood love of snow, discover a hardiness of soul I imagined I had acquired over the eighteen Midwestern winters I endured before migrating south, and face the cold with steely determination. But nothing prepared me for the minus thirty-degree wind chills and the gray. I never missed a day of school growing up because it was too cold, yet cold is the reason for most of the ones my children miss.

And the gray. Did I mention that? As I recall, the sun still shone during Indiana winters.

But the children are in school today, and the birds are confused, prematurely compelled to gather string and straw and hair for nests, and the daffodils are inching their way above ground sooner than any horticulturalist would advise. *Carpe diem*, as they say. And we are seizing the day, taking advantage of the weather and a week off in my teaching schedule for a walk, just the two of us.

Ginger is thinking about going back to work. She pastored churches for twelve years, then took two and a half years off when we moved here to help our family get settled and to recover from the weariness of full-time ministry. She's not convinced the recovery is over, but the challenge of raising three children on one salary suggests maybe it should be. A church close to where we live is looking for someone to coordinate their worship. It's an administrative position Ginger could do with her eyes closed, and they've offered her the job.

These are the things we talk about as we walk. I feel like we're the two on the road to Emmaus after the Resurrection in the Gospel of Luke: two confused disciples, trying to puzzle out what's next. But for Ginger it goes deeper than the simple either-or of taking the job or not. The process creates a deeper kind of questioning about identity: Who am I after the work I've done? If I take an administrative job, will people value my experience as a pastor? How would I feel as a staff person when I supervised the staff in my last position? Is this the right kind of work for me?

They are questions I can't answer. But I can walk next to Ginger and join the woods in their silent listening, in their settled companioning. I can give her the space to name these puzzles of self-knowledge.

We end up sitting on a bench behind the nature center under a tree from which the warmth is trying to coax new leaves. We face the meadow of Canada thistle, dotted with a couple of trees in which birds can pause on their ventures across the meadow. Beyond the meadow lies the pond, and surrounding the meadow and the pond is an amphitheater of trees that projects nature's few afternoon sounds.

"I can't believe I've lived for four decades, and I still don't know who I am," Ginger says with a note of sadness in her voice, as if knowing who she is would help her make a decision.

A red-tailed hawk springs into flight from the trees just beyond the pond, soars into the sky and toward us, gliding over the meadow, screeching his call, which is answered by a hawk in the woods behind us. I think, *Hawks don't ask why they are here, or what they should do next. They are driven by the forces of evolution and instinct; they don't ever need to discern. They don't ask, "Does this screech sound like the real me?"*

———

Each year I ask the students in my introductory spirituality course to read an essay by Thomas Merton called "Things in Their Identity," then write a paper to demonstrate they get what he's talking about. And each year a number of students make the same mistake.

They make the mistake because they love his opening image, and because his prose is poetic and inconsistent and meandering—it's not always clear he knows what he's talking about. But mostly they do it because he seduces them with the image of a tree glorifying God simply by being itself. It can do no other, for a "tree imitates God by being a tree." "The forms and individual characters of living and growing things, of inanimate beings, of animals and flowers and all nature, constitute their holiness in the sight of God," Merton writes—which means he could have begun with the red-tailed hawk, or the stately black oak, or this prematurely budding tree that canopies the bench Ginger and I are sharing.

And because so many of my students have absorbed the shallow wisdom of the culture—just be yourself—they see Merton pointing to nature being itself and assume he must be making an analogy. Here, I imagine them thinking, the greatest spiritual writer of the twentieth century is confirming the one truth I've been told since childhood: I just need to be me. By being like the tree, by being who I naturally am, by being what God has made me to be, I glorify God; I reflect God's image.

This assumption that they know what he's about to say keeps them from seeing two key words (or maybe they stop reading before they get to them): "But . . . unlike." He offers that whole bit about the tree, as beautiful and compelling and perhaps true as it is, for the sake of contrast. His point is how we are *not* like the tree, the flower, the rock, the hawk. His point is that humans are *different*.

> Unlike the animals and the trees, it is not enough for us to be what our nature intends. It is not enough for us to be individual [human beings]. For us, holiness is more than humanity.
>
> Our vocation is not simply to *be*, but to work together with God in the creation of our own life, our own identity, our own destiny. We are free beings and [children] of God. . . . To put it better, we have been called to share with God the work of *creating* the truth of our identity.

How much easier to be the hawk, or the tree! To live, even for a few moments, without choices or questions or identity crises. To blissfully know (or blissfully not know) who or what you are and simply do what nature intends. What a relief.

The "but . . . unlike" is a summons, and it haunts me. It means our choosing matters. Our selection of a college major, our choice of jobs, our decisions to move, the games we play in the workplace to situate ourselves for advancement, the giving in or not to the impulse to shout at people in traffic; deciding whether to vent to a colleague about another colleague who has frustrated you, or whine to the dean, or confront the other colleague, or let it go—none of these is a benign choice. Each is a chance to participate with God in my becoming myself.

Or not—because sometimes venting feels so good.

I have my arm around Ginger as we sit on the bench in the afternoon sun. We are living in the "but . . . unlike," dwelling there. We all are, or can be, in these decades called midlife. It's a haunting place, full of questions, tinted with confusion, tattooed with doubt. But it has this advantage: it's not a small place. You can breathe here. It's wide as the hawk-traced sky.

Here's what's small, constricting: the identities we create for ourselves. Those are tiny rooms, really, basically cupboards under the staircase. They are so small we even hesitate when we think about inviting God in to participate with *us* in the creation of our lives, identities, destinies. We are the stars of the shows we stage in these rooms, and God sometimes gets a cameo.

Midlife gives us a chance to shift into the spacious life of God, and accept the invitation to participate with God in creating who we can become, rather than settling down and living the rest of our lives in the tiny houses of what we have made ourselves to be.

I don't know what that looks like. I don't know how it answers the question, "Should I take this job?" I suspect it relates to letting go of our attachments, or at least acknowledging them, because attachments are the walls of the tiny house, as well as the bars over the windows, bars we affixed to the thick, brick walls for protection from intruders, but have turned into prison bars, confining us to our self-made identities.

Living the next forty years in such a prison, defending from insult and injury and slight, fixing every crack, filling every crevice, caulking, caulking, caulking away to seal it airtight—it feels hopeless, exhausting.

Dwelling in the territory of "but . . . unlike" means attending to work that hawks and trees, flowers and bees, get to ignore—work that is uniquely human. Maybe, when this work gets underway, it becomes easier to know what comes next. Maybe it becomes easier to see the choices we're given as invitations to join God in art class and paint together the picture of who we're meant to be.

What Dan Said

Dan and I taught together at a retreat in Louisiana a few years ago; that's where we met. He began each lecture with five minutes of silence. His lanky figure bent itself onto a too-small plastic chair facing the rest of us, his face went serene and his eyes closed, his long fingers rested splayed on his thighs. He didn't tell us what to do. Some of us just watched him, and others, I suspect, dared inch toward the edges of the silence with which he was so well acquainted.

I don't remember the official topic of his talks—we retreat presenters have a way of molding any assigned topic to fit what we really want to discuss—but I remember his espousing what he called a "do-nothing" theory of leadership that I have some sympathy with, a Quakerish approach that says leaders and communities should wait in openness and silence, inhabiting a kind of stillness in their life together, until a way forward emerges—which it undoubtedly would, he told us.

I took few walks at the retreat center, deterred by signs warning of alligators. But now that Dan is visiting Pittsburgh, we take a walk together.

Dan is taller than I am. His long strides force me to clip along at a faster pace than usual, especially downhill. I'm seizing this opportunity to pick the brain of a man who has spent time—long hours, days, weeks—exploring the depths of silence. I want to know how far into those depths you can go, and what—or whom—you find there. Since everything I've read suggests such soul-spelunking can be painful, frightening—Rowan Williams calls this pain the "anguish of confronting an inner landscape in which, when you look honestly, there seems no hope of getting it in order"—I thought, why not ask someone who has been there before going there myself, the way you might ask someone how terrifying the roller coaster is before taking your place in line? So, I invited Dan to join me on my walk.

You wouldn't take Dan for a guru. A Minnesotan, he looks more like someone you'd find leading an Alaskan expedition than offering spiritual direction or teaching meditation. He e-mailed me a couple months earlier to see if he could crash at our house for a night while he traveled back home from West Virginia. When he arrived last night, the sun had nearly set, and our little dog, just at the beginning of his growing skittishness with strangers, barked ferociously at Dan's shadowed form traipsing down the hill in our front yard.

As we walk, I ask him about contemplation, about meditation. I tell him that when I talk to others about contemplation, I say it's like resting in God, like crawling into the lap of Love; that I usually point to Psalm 131, with its image of the soul as a weaned child pressing against its mother's breast, not wanting anything but her presence; I say it's like finding home. As I'm speaking, I can't remember if I know this from my own experience, or because I've been reading about it and writing about it and teaching about it for so long that I've come to confuse the words and descriptions with the experience itself, though I don't tell Dan this.

He says: Yes, it's that—rest in God. But it's not that alone. Something comes before.

He says: It's also self-discovery. There's so much white noise—the shallow perseverations about our attachments, usually to false images of ourselves.

He says: Meditation helps you see the falseness, the falseness that blocks access to your truest self.

He says: Only *that* self can rest in God, because only that self is real.

A Jewel from the Deep

Mary Clare leads the way again, this time with a map in hand, which she unfolds and inspects frequently. But the discovery she makes along the way is not indicated on the map; no grand "'X' marks the spot." Yet I need just this discovery to help me puzzle out how I might participate with God in the creation of my identity, in the discovery of my truest self, for what she finds reminds me of a word I already know.

We begin down Goldenrod, a trail that traces the west boundary of the meadow of Canada thistle, the two separated by a border of scraggly trees and brush, several of the trees stretching high enough to reach over the path and link arms with the trees on the opposite side. Their roots meet beneath the path, some emerging above ground, creating a tripping hazard. Past the meadow, Goldenrod curves around the west side of the pond and passes the pond along the north until it meets Spring Hollow at the pavilion. If you head straight where Goldenrod curves, you enter a wooded valley along a narrower path called Violet. A bench sits at the intersection of these two paths and looks over the pond toward the pavilion on the other side, a bat box hangs on a pole above the bench, and an upside-down rowboat rests for the winter season. As we walk along Goldenrod, Silas sticks close, intermittently holding my hand; Mary Clare stumbles on the exposed roots.

I am conscious that we are still in the season of Lent, the weeks before Easter given to examining our lives and confessing our sins and making small sacrifices that create some space for a new attentiveness to the mystery of God.

Until a couple of weeks ago, when Mary Clare presented us with the barbed hunting arrow, I wouldn't have thought of describing Lent as the season in which we devote ourselves to discovering and ridding our lives of attachments. Now I'm remembering that spiritual writer Ronald Rolheiser once observed that the paschal mystery—the mystery of Christ's dying and rising again—patterns the Christian spiritual life: the ongoing dying to the false self with its blinding attachments, and a rising to the true self that can see and follow better the path of love.

But that three-letter word still nags: *How?*

It used to feel so easy. Go on spiritual retreats and learn new practices: centering prayer, breath prayer, body prayer, *lectio divina*. Or give up sweets and chips for

Lent, the latter necessary for me when we lived in the country, where a church member's husband worked as a potato chip delivery man. He donated all of the recently or almost out-of-date chips to the cupboards in the church kitchen. Thirty yards away from our house, they called to me like sirens day and night, and only in Lent was I able to veer away from the jagged rocks.

Or embark on a project like, say, taking forty hikes in the year after I turn forty.

There was always something I could *do*, and I still do many of these things. But is that what Merton's idea of working with God in the creation of my identity is all about—engaging in a routine of spiritual calisthenics?

I love that my almost eleven-year-old boy still likes to hold my hand. The thought pleases me, the way it interrupts my rumination.

The kids like the fringes of the pond. Silas sits on the overturned rowboat, disturbing the water's shallow edge with a stick. The pond is drained in the winter, but melted snow and late winter rains have begun filling it again. The water level is still low enough that about three feet of shoreline can be investigated. As I watch Silas swirl the water, Mary Clare runs to me with her most recent discovery: two snail shells caked in dried dirt.

Later research will tell me that these are shells of one of two kinds of snail, either the brown mystery snail, the aquatic snail native to this region, or the Chinese mystery snail, an invasive species introduced to North America in 1890, which looks nearly identical. On average the invasive variety is larger, but both snails are brown, their whorls spiraling to a point. The ones Mary Clare hands me are over an inch long, and through the mud I can see the faint black streaks that run perpendicular to the spiral.

I stand with these dirty shells cradled in my hands. While Mary Clare begs to take them home, I remember another image of Merton's: "The true inner self must be drawn up like a jewel from the bottom of the sea, rescued from the confusion, from indistinction, from immersion in the common, the nondescript, the trivial, the sordid."

I can see the jewel in my mind, just as I can handle these mystery shells. The jewel can't find itself. The jewel waits in the murky depths to be raised, cleansed of seaweed and cleared of barnacles, so it can capture the light, reflect and refract it, as it is meant to do. As only it can.

I am this shell, that jewel. Waiting to be found. Needing to be cleansed and polished. Wanting to be discovered. I can't make finding myself a project, can't confidently claim my role as God's partner. There is only one thing I can do. Since I've tried everything else, one option remains: to consent.

In less than two weeks, there will be a confluence that is the solar eclipse of the Christian calendar, a real rarity: March 25, the Feast of the Annunciation, the day the angel Gabriel announced to Mary that she would bear Christ, and Good Friday, the day of Christ's crucifixion, will share the same square on the calendar, which won't happen again until the year 2157. On the same day, Christians will observe the day of Christ's conception and the day of his death, the two days that tell us most emphatically that consent is the heart of the Christian spiritual life: Mary's "let it be with me," the model of consent; Christ's "not my will but thine," the flowering of consent.

The necessity of consent strikes me with a certain force in this threshold of discovery, in this crossing over to midlife, for what do we do during the first half of life but live willfully? We work to make something of ourselves, make a name for ourselves. We build the shell we anticipate living in the rest of our lives, a sturdy, strong, impenetrable shell we call *myself*. I know that's what I've done.

Maybe this is why when I speak on contemplative spirituality—a posture of prayer that values receptivity over acquisition—the groups rarely include people in their twenties and thirties. Maybe those folks are so busy with their careers and families and projects they don't have time to come. But now I wonder: maybe, given the shape of our life projects in the first four decades, we don't see the value. We are making ourselves. The idea that our truest identity is something we receive—how could that be?

Yet it seems so clear to me now. My work with God is the hard work of letting go of the idea that I'm the one who does the work. Can my path—as I continue to grow into my vocation to love, my vocation to be me—be marked by consent, by a willed passivity that seeks to allow God to show the *real* me to myself? Can it allow God to reveal to me the multiple, intricate, beautiful facets of the jewel that I am, however long it takes?

Happy to see the shells go into my pocket, Mary Clare consults her map and points us forward onto the trail called Violet. She's on the trail before Silas rises from his perch on the rowboat, a trail much darker, much narrower, and, I know, more treacherous than the rooty Goldenrod.

I consent to follow Mary Clare, whom we have named after Mary, the mother of the way of consent. I consent to take Silas's hand, to allow his narrow fingers to interlace with mine, and to enjoy the rush of endorphins this filial intimacy releases. And I consent to walk into the wilderness of self-discovery with this One in whom my faith has recently ebbed and flowed, but now seems to flow in longing, hope, and love.

— TRAIL THREE —

Finding Fruitfulness
in the Second Half

We need to remind ourselves that Jesus never suggested that we should evaluate the health of his people by how much power they wielded or how much privilege they amassed. Rather, Jesus insisted that his followers would be identifiable as his followers by their fruit.

–Philip Kenneson

April Is Bustin' Out All Over

I know better than to anthropomorphize, to project upon these winged wonders human characteristics like the experience of falling in love, like suffering those first pangs and delights of romance that make middle schoolers across the land forget their names and their lunchboxes and their way around school halls; those sensations that compel folks in their twenties and thirties to buy rings and take vows before these flutters have a chance to settle into the routine pangs and delights of a life together over the long haul. But I can't help it; it's spring.

I see a male eastern towhee, one of the few birds I can't forget from my bird-watching days because of its distinctive coloration: rufous feathers beneath white-tipped black wings, black head and back, and an eerie rufous iris encircling the pupil. He ascends from the ground into a tangle of vines around a tree, then shimmies out of the tangle, gets a foothold, and sings. I can't help but think, *Is he singing to attract a mate, or are these notes of joy for having already found one?* I can't help but see him as a feathered Romeo, singing, "Did my heart love till now? Foreswear it, sight! / For I ne'er saw true beauty till this night."

And I can't help but wonder, *In what region of his brain are the neurons firing?* That's because, on the way to my walk this April afternoon, I heard a radio story about a neuroscientist who researches romantic love. He slides test subjects into MRI machines, prompts them to think romantic thoughts, and then observes what areas of the brain "light up" with activity. This activity occurs, it turns out, in the old reptilian part of the brain, what the researcher called the "survival" part, right next to hunger and thirst. Romance serves an evolutionary purpose: it initiates the mating that transmits genes to offspring and preserves the species.

Now I see: two robins building a nest, their tiny reptilian brains no doubt lighting up as they play house. And now: two cardinals, a bright male and drab female, singing to each other, call and response—signs of the evolutionary necessity that we humans, thanks to the burden of consciousness and the gift of language, have learned to call romance.

A line from the musical *Carousel*'s song "June is Bustin' out All Over" pops into my head: "Love has found my brother Junior, and my sister's even loonier, and my ma is getting kittenish with pap—because it's June!" And I think, *We must start things sooner in Pittsburgh.*

A theologian might put this whole business differently than the neuroscientist, might say that in spring nature is heeding the primordial summons of God to "be fruitful and multiply"—a commandment I have dutifully honored.

I've done my part to bring three children into the world, a part which I admit is dwarfed by Ginger's contribution. "Sire," I believe, is the word for my contribution, along with offering moral support for nine months and in the delivery room. When our first was born, my tasks as sire included: to hold the swaddled boy, to sing to him the lullaby he'd already heard a thousand times through a sea of amniotic fluid, and to tell him his name. "You are Simeon," I said, at which moment I felt like the Simeon he was named after, the old man in the Bible who extended his arms to hold baby Jesus at the temple, who saw in him more than anybody else could see. Then I carried my Simeon to Ginger and watched her hold him to her chest.

These days, though, I'm not thinking about that kind of fruitfulness. I'm thinking about another kind, noticing the midlife urge to pass along more than my genes in this world.

Jesus said to be fruitful, but he wasn't talking about procreation in the book-of-Genesis sense, with its whole chapters devoted to begetting. He was talking about living a fruitful life, a life from which the fruits of love and service and self-sacrifice might spring, a life that comes from an intimate union with our divine Source. "Those who abide in me and I in them bear much fruit," he said.

I'm not surprised that I'm thinking about this fruitfulness now, because Jesus also said such a harvest only follows pruning, when the divine vinedresser trims the dead branches of our attachments, plucking "the world from our hearts," as Thomas Kelly put it. By "world," Kelly meant the egoistical pursuit of images of ourselves many of us spend the first decades of life conjuring, establishing, and defending. While I'm sure many dead-branch attachments still have to be clipped from my life, I know a little about what it is to see those images for what they are—illusions—and watch them vanish, dissolve like sandcastles at high tide.

The year before I moved to Pittsburgh to become a seminary professor, I twice failed to become the dean of something. Being a dean—of a divinity school, of a university chapel, of *something*—was a fantasy I'd nurtured for years. The first time, I failed because the stress of the selection process triggered one of the worst anxiety attacks of my life the morning of the interview, and I couldn't recover sufficiently by the time of interview—held in a stately glass room of an art museum, where a committee of university elites grilled me for three hours—to do my best.

The second time was the more revealing. I'd been offered the job of dean of the chapel at a small university, a job I thought I wanted until my conversation alone with the university president. He seemed to me a man I couldn't trust—manipulative, egotistical, dictatorial. I walked out of his palatial office suite, decorated with images of the many self-help books he'd authored, questioning if I could work there.

When the job offer came, I did my best to discern, and in the end, when I'd decided to take the job, I told Ginger, "At least I will be called the dean of something." Even as the words left my mouth, I sensed their shallowness, their vacuity; I tasted the bitter flavor of my false self.

The next week, during the negotiations around salary, the provost told me they'd decided to change the job title to "Minister to the University." And I balked. I thought, *I'll be damned if I'm going to take a job I don't want and get demoted before stepping foot on campus.*

When I called to decline the offer, I wished it had been because I couldn't imagine working for an institution I didn't trust, that didn't shoot straight with me, but I knew what I was doing: backing out of a job I didn't want but had already agreed to take because it promised to be an ego-satisfying promotion. With this exposure of the hollowness of my soul came a kind of gladness after the shame. This pruning, after all, this stripping away of some illusions I'd had of myself, might make some space for another kind of fruitfulness, more like the fruit the Apostle Paul commends, fruit that also comes from a relationship with the Source of life: love, joy, peace, patience, kindness, goodness, faithfulness, gentleness, and self-control.

As I walk, I jump when I hear rustling in the brush next to me. I see motion, flashes of brown out of the corner of my eye, and I imagine a bear rising up to devour me. Instead I see six goofy turkeys—three male turkeys chasing three female turkeys, visions of fruitfulness no doubt dancing in the males' heads as they strut along, showing off for the playing-hard-to-get females.

All I have to do is look into the blue eyes of Simeon or Mary Clare, or to see my own shyness in Silas, to know I have successfully passed along my genes. I've done at least that much for the species. But these walks are making space for me to ask other questions: What should fruitfulness look like in my life *now*? Am I close enough to my divine Source for another kind of fruit to be born through me? Will my fruit be born in the classroom—is that where I'm supposed to be fruitful? Is my fruitfulness in making lunches every day for these three kids even when I'd rather be praying or sleeping or reading or writing? How will the fruits that Paul lists become embodied in my life? How long will it take them to ripen? What will be their shape, their color, their flavor—how sour, how sweet?

I trust that my own longing to be fruitful and multiply in this broader, figurative, sense indicates that my season of begetting is not over.

WALK 9

A Word That Names What I Want

At eight o'clock on a cool April morning, the sun has not risen high enough to warm the bench I sit on, located on the path ironically named Vista. Though the path runs across the top ledge of a shallow valley, the valley itself is overgrown, so that rather than enjoying the view, I am gazing into a wall of brush and weeds and teenage trees a few feet in front of me and several feet high. I'm sitting here thinking of a word, a word I never much paid attention to until I attended an academic conference in Dayton, Ohio, last December, shortly before my fortieth birthday, a word this bench has reminded me of.

Since attending this conference was a way to fund a trip to see my mother in Indiana, I didn't expect to hear a presentation that would offer a nugget so juicy I'm still chewing on it. A woman finishing a PhD in I-don't-remember-what was reporting on the work of John Kotre, a psychologist who researches human development. His work builds on the seminal thoughts of Erik Erikson, who, in the 1950s, coined the word "generativity." Erikson, one of the first psychologists to divide human development into distinct stages, said that between the ages of forty and sixty-five humans take a generative turn. We become less obsessed with achievement and success and more interested in passing on wisdom, gifts, and blessing to our community, especially to younger generations. In short, we begin to yearn to contribute to the flourishing of others: generativity.

Kotre, according to the presenter, builds on the work of Erikson by making a distinction between two types of generativity. "There's a kind of generativity that produces something primarily for the aggrandizement of the maker. Kotre calls this 'agentic generativity,'" said the presenter. I wrote it down and wished I'd had a dictionary to look up "agentic."

"The other kind he calls 'communal generativity.' That's just the opposite. It's produced for others, not out of self-concern." She finished her talk and sat down at a table, where a senior scholar sat ready to offer a response. But I didn't hear anything else said. Her words were enough for me.

The bench I'm sitting on is the fruit of an Eagle Scout project. In order to achieve the highest scouting rank possible, a young scout has to lead others in making something that will benefit his community. That's generativity. He gets rewarded the rank of Eagle Scout, which is practically synonymous with "upstanding citizen." So, does that make his work *agentic* generativity, with its blend of gift and self-concern?

I hated Cub Scouts—I didn't make it any farther than that—and have saved my faux silver Cub Scout ring to remind me never to do this to my boys. But someone liked it enough to earn perhaps more than a hundred Boy Scout badges, then additional Eagle Scout badges, then rally some friends to build a few benches and place them around this nature reserve, including here on the narrow Vista trail facing a façade of brush and weeds, the perfect place to ponder the journey from a life focused on achieving badges and accolades and recognition to a life centered on using my gifts for others, passing along any wisdom I might have for the good of my community and those younger than I.

It occurs to me that it's probably not an either-or. Those psychological divisions of human development have no hard-and-fast transitions between them. I suspect many of us inhabit more than one region at a time. Will I ever lose self-concern, ever finally be done with thinking about what people are thinking about me? Probably not, but I want to respond to the yearning to let it go—an urge which I now understand is not uncommon for people my age.

———

Pastor Tom called this week. I preached at our church last November when he was out of town, and someone, it seems, remembered my sermon. The two thousand words I cobbled together out of my imagination, a little research, and my own fledgling faith mattered to someone, helped remind him that *he* matters—no small thing. Especially since I had every reason to believe the sermon was a dud.

I preached on the passage in Genesis that depicts Jacob's famous dream with the ladder and the angels ascending and descending, and the unmistakable presence of the Lord, all while Jacob slept in no-man's land with his head on a stone. After he woke, the experience of God's presence was so vivid he took his pillow-stone and set it up as a pillar, doused it with oil, and named the place Bethel, "House of God." He uttered one of the most memorable lines in Scripture: "Surely the Lord is in this place—and I did not know it!"

I said, "This means you don't need to go out of your way to track God down. You don't need to go on a thin-places tour of Ireland, or spend a week fasting at a monastery in the deserts of Arizona. God is with you wherever you are. Every place can be the house of God."

I was saying this to a congregation, but I was really preaching to myself, reminding myself of what I believed at some level, even though I sometimes waffle, sometimes find it hard to notice the signs of God's presence, and rarely wake up and exclaim with the confidence of Jacob. I was saying, "Roger, God is with you."

After the sermon, I invited each parishioner to receive a small stone as a reminder of what Jacob knew and most of us long to know: the Love that made all that is will never leave us alone. *God is with us.*

Two days later I ran into one of the more attentive, thoughtful members of the congregation at a park. I was pushing Mary Clare on a swing; I don't know what Barbara was doing, because her kids had outgrown swings.

"I enjoyed your sermon Sunday, but I forget—what was the rock supposed so symbolize?" In other words: *sermon fail.* Good thing I was preaching to myself as well, because I might have been the only one who got the message.

So it was a pleasant surprise when Pastor Tom called to tell me that a young man in the congregation, a painter, had so taken the message of the sermon to heart that it had inspired a painting, and he'd entered the painting into a juried art exhibit and won first place.

"As a preacher, I know we so rarely hear when our words make a difference—we're more likely to hear complaints—so I thought you'd like to know," Tom said.

On my way home that afternoon I stopped by the art exhibit. The painting, entitled "Bethel," hung amidst the other entrants. It was a large piece, about one yard square, of a two-toned gray stone nestled in swirling grass, each blade painted with precision. The stone looked completely ordinary, mundane. It didn't resemble a religious monument, or an altar, or a marker memorializing a mystical experience. It was just a normal stone that reminded Jacob, and me, and—through my sermon—this young artist, that God is here.

And, through the young artist, I was reminded again.

Now I wonder, having left the Eagle Scout bench to continue my walk: maybe that is what generativity looks like—nothing special, nothing out of the ordinary. My stringing together a few words, the meaning of which landed in the heart of another and inspired his generative act, so that the message continues, no longer in the form of words, but in brush strokes and paint hues and whatever the imagination of the viewer makes of them.

Perhaps this is what generativity feels like: no badge, no honors ceremony, just a secret a few of us know, and a sense of satisfaction, of failure redeemed.

WALK 10

Saints of the Second Half

Ignatius of Loyola: thirty when he had his conversion from a life of the twin pursuits of military glory and the attention of the ladies to a life devoted to the vocation of "helping souls," and fifty when he founded the Society of Jesus, the Jesuits, which numbered adherents in the thousands at his death.

Teresa of Avila: forty-seven when she finally abandoned her comfort in the lax convent where she lived and set about reforming her order, establishing seventeen new convents in the last twenty years of her life.

Thomas Merton: twenty-six when he entered the monastery, but fifty when he became a hermit, a transition which began a most generative period of his life, when he was extraordinarily prolific, and his attention turned to diagnosing the racial ills in American society and supporting civil rights and anti-war activists like Daniel Berrigan, among others.

Jean Vanier: thirty-six when he moved into a small house with Raphael and Philippe, two men both mentally and physically disabled, who had lived in a psychiatric institution, with no agenda other than to love them and share life with them. He named the house L'Arche, which means "The Ark." Today, 149 L'Arche communities around the world welcome men and women with severe mental and physical disabilities, many of whom have been rejected by their families and society.

I dub folks like this "saints of the second half"—people who, later in life, turned outward in service, discovered new vocations, accomplished remarkable feats, some of them renewing or founding institutions that continue to impact the globe.

Sometimes, when I wonder what great thing I will accomplish for others in the second half of my life, and then doubt that I ever will, it's helpful for me to remember that none of those above married or raised children. Perhaps I should stop thinking of great things; generativity does not equal greatness. A sermon preached and remembered. A class taught. A book written. A confused soul advised. Could this be the shape of my generativity? Could this be what it means for me to be a saint of the second-half?

And how about: three children loved and fed and taught?

Today Silas wears his tie-dyed shirt that matches the hacky-sack he's pocketed for the walk. Simeon wears his signature orange sweatshirt and orange shorts, and Mary Clare, a long-sleeved pink and white striped shirt, blue jeans, and a green braided leather belt she claims looks fashionable. Simeon also carries his own staff, a stick that he found and painted gold and brown, which looks like a cross between Moses's staff and Pharaoh's scepter; he could play either the Hebrews' sea-splitting savior or the tyrant in hot pursuit. He may not want to play either of them, though. Maybe he carries the staff because he wants to be like *me*.

Silas kicks the hacky-sack because I taught him how. I bought the one he carries in Mexico years ago. In college after choir practice, Matt, Norberto, and I volleyed a hacky-sack from ankle to knee to thigh to chest for fifteen minutes before dinner. Now Silas is my partner.

When we pass the dogwood tree with its white flowers, and I start to sing, ". . . Blossoms of snow may you bloom and grow, bloom and grow, forever," Mary Clare joins me on the next line—"Edelweiss, Edelweiss"—because lately she's been sitting with me at the piano, learning the musicals I love.

These walks give me the unstructured time to be with them—sometimes all together, sometimes individually—to see what they are learning, to discern who or what is molding their character, and to hear from them. They also give time to pass along what little wisdom I've gained over forty years and to share crucial bits of knowledge that will help them navigate their world—like the fact that Andrew Lloyd Webber should have killed the idea for a sequel to *The Phantom of the Opera* before it grew into the disaster that it is (the Phantom on Coney Island? *Come on!*)—a conviction each of my children now shares.

This is the kind of stuff parents of twelve-, ten-, and six-year-olds get to do now that we're past the parenting stage concerned primarily with keeping them alive. We get to help them see what real living looks like, at least as much as we've figured it out. Who knows? When they're forty, something I said or did might come back to them. Who knows? Maybe they'll take a few walks and pass on wisdom to the youngsters in their lives.

Unless they are busy becoming the next Ignatius, Teresa, Merton, or Vanier, spending the second half of their lives renewing the institutions or starting the movements that will change the world. Either way, I hope I'm alive to see it.

WALK 11

Let It Rain

My arthritis is telling me a front is moving through; rain is on the way. I drop Silas off at his friend Daniel's birthday party, armed with the crudely wrapped gift he has chosen: the children's novel *Pax*, a book I recently read and recommended to Silas. In it a boy's father forces him to release his pet fox because the dad is going off to serve in the army, and the boy is moving in with his grandfather. The book follows the boy on his own adventure to find his fox, and discover himself along the way. I believe when Silas was on the last page I saw a tear tumbling down his cheek, but I didn't mention it, didn't want to make him self-conscious. I know he saw me teary-eyed when I got the end, though not weeping like I did at the end of *Bridge to Terabithia*. I feel no small amount of parenting pride that I can read and be moved by a book, imagine that Silas might like it, and discover he likes it enough he wants to share it with his friends. *An example of generativity?* I wonder, as he hops out of the car.

I take a now familiar route down Spring Hollow and into the valley. Just past the pond, where Spring Hollow begins to narrow and the Oak Forest trail veers off to the right into a region still uncharted by me, a chipmunk scurries to the base of a stump, stares at me, then dashes up the stump and dives into a hole.

What is starkly obvious to me: green. A week ago the maple leaves had just begun to open, still translucent and fringed with copper. Now a lime green canopy overhangs me, festive leaves celebrating their emergence, like debutantes showing off at a ball.

When I reach the bench next to Harts Run, I can't sit and be soothed by the trickle because two young lovers are embracing on the bench. They part suddenly when they hear my approach. "Do you know how to get to the tree-top lookout?" they ask. I do, and I tell them, and then feel some satisfaction that I look like someone who has been here enough to know the lay of the land.

Since the couple turns left to follow Spring Hollow, I continue straight onto Woodlawn, the trail Mary Clare accidently led us onto last month. Then you could barely tell where the edge of the path met the unkempt ground, the brown dirt of the trail segueing seamlessly into the dead winter brush. But today the spring growth presses onto the path and narrows it, and I dodge poison ivy and prehistoric–looking ferns pushing through the groundcover. It occurs to me that rain, like the rain

I'm hurrying to beat, has occasioned this burst of growth, this reemergence of life, so sudden, new, unexpected despite its annual recurrence.

I think of Psalm 65, a psalm usually associated with the fall, the harvest season. The psalm celebrates abundance. "You crown the year with your bounty," the psalmist says to God. To this day I can't read this psalm without picturing the church my wife served as an associate pastor before we were married, where I had the dubious distinction of being the pastor's boyfriend. Each year in October the front lawn was transformed into a sea of squash; the youth sold pumpkins to fund their spring mission trip. An abundance of pumpkins crowned the lawn, as if a tidal wave of orange had crashed in front of the church. These pumpkins: an image of fall's bounty.

But before bounty, rain, the psalm declares:

> *You visit the earth and water it,*
> *   you greatly enrich it.*
> *You water its furrows abundantly,*
> *   settling its ridges,*
> *softening it with showers,*
> *   and blessing its growth.*

Rain—the rain I'm trying to outrun—fuels creation's own selfless generativity. It falls with no concern for itself, doing only what's in its nature to do: seep through the siphon of soil to roots awaiting water. And with the water and the warmth of the sun and all of nature's other signals of the season, the dormant plants awaken and say, "It's time—time to show the world what we've got."

Sometimes Christians sing to the Holy Spirit, imagining the Spirit as rain:

> *Spirit of the Living God, fall afresh on me.*

And when we sing this, we're affirming that God's very heart is communal generativity, creativity without self-regard, Life bestowing life without thought for itself. The Spirit in Genesis broods over the chaos and partners with God to bring about creation, until it becomes clear that this Spirit *is* Life-giving God. God, like rain, brings forth life and offers life abundant to what already lives.

In the Church year, we are between Easter and Pentecost. On the first Easter, in the evening, Jesus appeared to his frightened disciples in the upper room. I imagine them huddled together in a corner with the doors locked, afraid of the Powers That Be. That kind of existence feels familiar to me: huddled, defensive, self-protective, with no possibility of sharing with others, of unreserved self-giving in love.

Then the One they recently loved and lost appears in their midst, locked door notwithstanding, and breathes on them the Holy Spirit—an act preacher Fred Craddock calls the "quiet" Pentecost—freeing them to share the love and life that they had experienced through relationship with this One with a world huddled in a corner, afraid.

Not long after, the loud Pentecost happens, with the Spirit falling like an April rain in Pittsburgh: torrentially. The ones present who receive *this* rain of God's life and energy and hope called Spirit become the ones who share with others this same life and energy and hope.

And they still do today. They write a song or preach a sermon or paint a picture that might, in our moments of doubt, breathe Spirit onto us and remind us what can be, and who *we* can be: participants in God's own generativity.

We can be rain.

———————————

The darker clouds approach quickly, the breeze picks up. But I no longer hurry. In fact, I begin to hope it does rain, that I become drenched in this life-giving water. I hope that I, like the first disciples, become rain, become a life at one with the divine generativity that can't stop giving, can't stop blessing, can't stop pouring love on this world. This image holds the answer to my question of late: in what part of my life will this longing for generativity be fulfilled—writing, parenting, preaching, *what*?

I've been reading a new book by Barbara Bradley Hagerty, former religions correspondent for NPR, on thriving in midlife. She discusses generativity, but reduces it to volunteerism as a strategy for happiness and long life. Some research suggests that when people volunteer in a capacity that matches their gifts they live longer. But it doesn't promote longevity if you volunteer against the grain of your gifts and personality. There's no payoff. The moral: strategize your midlife generatively wisely.

But something feels wrong to me about generativity being a strategy for happiness and length of years. Even more, I don't think generativity can be compartmentalized, reduced to the category of volunteering. We can't just check off the "generativity box" by ringing a bell outside of a store around Christmas, serving meals at a soup kitchen, or Christmas caroling at a nursing home—however worthy these activities in themselves. I don't want gift-giving, blessing-offering, and hope-providing to be a *part* of my life, added onto successful parenting, career advancement, and leisure pursuits. I want them to be my life. Period.

———————————

My tires crunch the gravel of the parking lot as I back out of my space, and the first drops of rain splatter on my windshield, exploding like water balloons. I've missed it; I'll arrive home dry. But I can imagine the earth and plants and trees opening themselves and turning toward the rain, the rain doing what it knows to do, and these earthbound plants doing what they know to do: receive, give thanks, and then grow the leaves, flowers, and fruit that decorate this patch of creation.

I want to join them, so I open my window, stick out my hand, and feel the whipping wind and the pelting rain the rest of the way home.

— TRAIL FOUR —

Learning to Pay Attention Anew

One of the biggest differences between the expert birder and the novice is that the expert has spent years training to see the details. The beginner must literally learn how to see them.

–David Sibley

Listen to your life. See it for the fathomless mystery that it is. In the boredom and pain of it no less than in the excitement and gladness: touch, taste, smell your way to the holy and hidden heart of it because in the last analysis all moments are key moments, and life itself is grace.

–Frederick Buechner

WALK 12

Watching Birds, Looking for God

Two tasks awaited me before this walk, before my re-education in attention. The first—fix the binoculars.

I've only dabbled in birdwatching over the last few years. My binoculars rest on a corner table in the dining room atop a stack of family prayer books, in case a bird worthy of note lands in the locust tree outside the dining room window. We've seen Baltimore orioles and pileated woodpeckers, both interesting enough to call the kids. Years have passed since I've birdwatched in earnest, but that's what I'm going to do these next few weeks, so I have some getting ready to do.

I'd had trouble focusing the binoculars the few times I'd used them recently. You don't need them for the pileated woodpeckers, which are the size of a crow, but you do for the orioles. We also like to watch the woodchucks in the backyard at 8X magnification, and the chipmunks dashing along the fence, tails perpendicular. But no adjustment I'd made had helped, until I remembered last fall, sitting crisscross-applesauce with the kids in the driveway, burning holes in leaves. We couldn't find a magnifying glass to focus the sunlight, so I unscrewed the binocular's two large lenses for us to use and begged the children not to scratch them.

I checked to see if I might have switched the lenses when I'd put them back on, if that might have been making me dizzy, though I didn't know why it would. And while I still don't know how binoculars work, I know now that it matters that the objective lenses, the big ones, stay with the left on the left, the right on the right—as I discovered when I switched them and could see clearly again. Task one—check.

I also needed to refresh my watching skills and remind myself what I was looking for and how to go about the looking. So early on this Saturday morning in May, before anyone else was awake, I pulled my *Sibley's Birding Basics* off the shelf, a book I hadn't touched in years, and began to read. Reading reminded me how I used to make a quick sketch of birds I didn't recognize to aid in later identification. It helped me recall how to behave "in the field"—to move quietly and gently, watching for movement, listening for sounds. And it reaffirmed that I should pay special attention both to markings around the head and to the relative size and shape of the bill.

As I skimmed the first couple chapters, eager get to the field, I began to think how reading that book was like reading books on prayer and life with God, which I also need if I'm going to learn to uncover what theologian Richard Lischer has called the hidden transcendence of God: "God is so transcendently *close* we cannot see him, and so woven into the fiber of things that he remains hidden, like the key that is 'lost' in plain view."

The prayer books on my shelves are like birding guides—books by experts telling the novice, "Look for *this*."

There is a whole world of life in the trees and the skies, and I didn't know anything about it until our friends Kim and Warren gave Ginger and me a birdfeeder as an engagement present. After we were married, I bought a shepherd's crook-hanger for the feeder, pressed it into the backyard of our rental house, hung the feeder, and filled it.

Then I started to pay attention. For the first time ever I looked forward to washing dishes, my nightly twenty minutes peering out the window, familiarizing myself with these unfamiliar visitors.

I also bought *The Sibley Guide to Birds*, and within a couple of months I'd identified almost forty species. They didn't all come to the feeder, but I began to look up and down and around. I fell in love with the gray catbird, meowing in the dense brush, with its steely gray body and darker tail and patch on its head, like the armor of a medieval knight, and with the eastern towhee—orange and black and white, with a quick backward hop to stir up insects.

On one of my favorite days, dozens of birds landed in the tops of the trees at the back of the yard. Unlike robins, which lean forward as they perch, these perched vertically. They leapt from the branches, hovered to nab insects, and flew back. With my binoculars, I could see their distinct crests, the black around their eyes like Catwoman's mask, and the markings that give them their name: the yellow and red at the tips of tail and wings, making them look dipped in wax. Hence, cedar waxwings, the most exotic bird I'd seen yet.

A gentle obsession developed. Each Saturday morning in those first months of marriage a mockingbird sang scat outside our bedroom window, and its song summoned me. I'd slip out of bed, grab my binoculars and hat, and walk to spy, observe, sketch, identify. A new hobby—that lasted about a year.

Because there were other things to do, too, things appropriate to what Carl Jung called the first half of life. Move from renting a house to buying a house. Finish a Ph.D. Get ordained. Have a kid, then another kid. Sell said house and move again. Develop a sense of accomplishment, a healthy ego. Strategize a prosperous future.

And, along the way, stop looking up, stop paying attention. Not only to the birds, but to a great deal else, as I had my gaze fixed at some point up ahead, on a picture of the life I wanted for myself and us.

That was thirteen years, three children, five houses, and two states ago—and something is saying to me: You are still strategizing the life you want, but what about the life you have *now*? Because "now" flies by; it doesn't last long.

I can't believe we are those parents, the ones who sit at the dinner table after the children have gone to play or read or stare at a screen, having forgotten *again* to take their dishes into the kitchen, parents who rest their chins in their hands and reminisce:

> *Remember when he couldn't sit still at the table, how often he ended up on the floor with his food? If we take a long blink, he will be in college.*
> *He was such a silly baby, and he's still got that wacky sense of humor.*
> *Can you believe how her big front teeth are growing in so fast? She's such a big girl now.*
> *Before you know it we'll be alone together again, just the two of us.*

What if Jung was right? What if, when I turned forty, a door was swinging open, inviting me into the second half of life, the half that's not about what's up ahead— not about building and creating and strategizing a life—but about learning to love the one I have, learning to be amazed day after day, the way I would be if a waxwing landed in the tree outside the dining room window, and I saw again that show-off with the mask and his flashy, waxy wings?

In other words: might it be time to pay attention again?

Perhaps by paying attention I can discover a unique aspect of a spirituality of midlife: that in midlife praying and living might come together, not as an asymptote, the two never meeting, but as a unity—praying and living, one act. If so, then noticing my wife and kids, my neighbors and colleagues without judgment—not fixing them or improving them or avoiding them, but being attentive to them—might be the path to seeing the love and mercy of God radiating from all that is.

However my convictions about God evolve in these next couple of decades, I don't ever want to say what the biblical patriarch Jacob said after sleeping out all night—after that famous dream with the ladder and the angels: "God was in this place, and I did not know it." If God is in this place, I want to know it.

I guess that means I need to learn to pay attention. Fortunately, I still have my binoculars, the bird books, and an Audubon nature reserve just miles from my house. What better place to practice?

The others are still asleep when I leave. I plan my walk as I drive. I will walk along an edge, along the path called Goldenrod, having just read that edges are good places to look for birds. To the right of this trail spreads a meadow with waist-high Canada thistle and a few trees; to its left rises an east-facing hill with dense brush and many trees. The hill catches the morning sun and should be a favorite spot for birds to snag breakfast. Goldenrod ends at a pond, so this short path affords views of three different habitats. Sibley has also reminded me of this: you don't need to cover lots of ground to see many birds, if you are patient.

I see, first, a pair of indigo buntings high in the maple tree in the middle of the meadow. These brilliant birds shine like phosphorescent beacons in the top of the tree, though Silas will later tell me he read somewhere that they are not really indigo at all, but black. (The first two articles in a Google search will suggest he's right: "Light Reflections Turn Black Bird into Indigo Bunting" and "Indigo Bunting's Color Is One of Nature's Tricks." But you wouldn't know it by looking.)

Equal to the pleasure of seeing flashes of indigo in the first few minutes is the thrill of seeing a bird I've never seen before, which I do minutes later. It flies over my head, from the meadow to a tree on the hillside, to forage for insects. It seems larger than a white-breasted nuthatch, but it moves headfirst down the tree, which surprises me. I had read once that only nuthatches do that—other birds back down trees. But I know this isn't a nuthatch. I note its predominate color, dark brown; the white stripes above each eye, the one in the middle of its head (I'm paying attention to the markings on the head); two white stripes on its wings and several others on its back and under its wings; and the relatively long, curved bill (*Not as long and curved as the brown creeper's*, I think, *though the markings are similar*). After it disappears, I make a sketch to help me recall these features later. I trust I will easily identify the bird, given its unusual motion on the tree. If finding God, that key lost in plain view, becomes this easy, then attentiveness to God in midlife will be simpler than I thought.

I will learn later today how wrong I am, when after half-an-hour of hunting I still can't find this bird in the book. Tomorrow, on my next walk, I will discover what I need to identify this bird and, with it, a clue to noticing the hidden transcendence of God so lightly, silently shimmering beneath the surface of things.

WALK 13

Warblers, Cheat Sheets, and Waffles

"Silas, wanna go birdwatching?" I've already been awake for a couple of hours when my son lumbers from his bedroom at seven.

"Yeah," he says, his hair sticking up in the back like the tail of a duck. He just turned eleven and is still game for many of my plans. Also, the children are not allowed to use their screens on Sunday mornings before church, so he might as well take an early walk with his dad on this crisp, clear May morning—Mother's Day— while the mother sleeps in. At least we won't have to fight for a place to park.

In the empty parking lot, Silas practices using my binoculars, aiming them at a chipping sparrow that hops around under a tree. While he's looking at it, I point out what he should notice—the dark stripe running through the eye, the white line above it, the cinnamon-colored patch on the head.

"You've got to pay attention to the distinctive markings on the head, because when you get home and look at the pages of sparrows in the field guide, they will all look the same." I remember Helen MacDonald's quip from *H Is for Hawk*, that ". . . bird-book illustrations never match the memory." I sketch the sparrow's head to show Silas how I note and remember the features that matter. *How quickly the skill returns*, I think. He stares at the bird, comparing it to my sketch, jaw hanging open in concentration.

We walk down Goldenrod toward the pond. There's a blue-gray gnatcatcher, finding a feast of gnats among the trees around the pond. Near the gnatcatcher, I see again the bird I failed to identify yesterday. Then it appeared brown and white, but this morning I can see it's black and white. It still walks headfirst down the tree, as if to mock me.

An older couple approaches us on Goldenrod, experienced birdwatchers—I don't need a book to identify them. Their binoculars look expensive, and each one wears a harness that wraps behind the back to relieve the strain of holding binoculars, necessary only for folks who birdwatch plenty. They are moving slowly, talking quietly, observing appropriate birding etiquette.

This morning I am not shy. "Can you help me identify a bird?" I ask. I describe the bird and tell them about my difficulty yesterday. "It was foraging like a warbler," I whisper, "but moved down the tree like a nuthatch."

"Warblers are hard, that's why I carry this cheat sheet," the woman says, pulling out of her pocket an identification guide, folded like an accordion, lamination peeling away from the edges and corners. She turns to the back panel and points to a black and white warbler, called, appropriately, black-and-white warbler. "Is that it?"

"Yes!" I exclaim, no longer *sotto voce*. Later in the afternoon, I will look up the bird in the *Sibley Guide* and note, with some pleasure, that this warbler walks down trees headfirst, making it easy, Sibley says, to misidentify as a nuthatch.

As Silas and I walk back to the car, I think about how nice it would be to have a cheat sheet for God, something in my pocket to help me notice that divine grandeur with which the earth is charged, as Gerard Manley Hopkins puts it. But I don't get one—I know that as truly as I know anything. And I'm satisfied.

I'm satisfied because I don't need one to help me feel the joy of sharing this morning with my son, appreciating his companionship and enthusiasm and willingness to learn. And I don't need a cheat sheet to tell me how helpful it is to find strangers on the journey who have been looking around and paying attention longer than I have, who can help me see what I've been missing. These two warbler-watchers remind me that even in midlife I am not alone, as the faces and names of friends flash through my mind—fellow pilgrims along these winding life trails. I make a mental note, a kind of midlife resolution, to be more open to others, those strangers along the way—potential angels, if the author of Hebrews is right—to open the house of my heart and let others in, to learn from those who have lived through more change with God than I can imagine, the guests in my life who have eyes and hearts more attuned to God's presence than mine.

When Silas and I get home, the table is set for a feast. Simeon has made a Mother's Day breakfast that he's putting on the table: Belgian waffles dusted with powdered sugar, topped with sliced bananas and strawberries and a dollop of freshly whipped cream. Ginger sits at the table, and Mary Clare is clambering into her seat. Silas dashes off to wash his hands.

And I stand still and notice it all, taking in this beautiful, chaotic tableau. I am paying attention to the moment, hoping Simone Weil is right, that attention is a kind of prayer; hoping the mystics are right, that God is in this moment; knowing either way: this is my life now, my life at forty, a life that, today, I'm happy to be stuck with.

WALK 14

Be a Body with a Head

After the Mother's Day breakfast last Sunday, we did what we usually do: went to church, where we observed Ascension Sunday. On that cloudless morning, blue sky visible through the clear sanctuary windows—out of which I've been known to practice birdwatching during sermons—we heard a middle schooler stumble through the New Testament reading from Acts, recounting Jesus's final conversation with his disciples, before a cloud lifted him into the sky, into heaven where he "sitteth at the right hand of the Father," as we say in the Creed. It's one of the passages that irritates the scientifically-minded folks in the congregation, with its pre-Copernican view of the universe, in which God and heaven are decidedly "up"—the view that dominated before we realized the earth is not the center of the universe and that there is no "up"—and with its mythological imagery of Jesus ascending on a cloud, like the apotheosis of George Washington in the Capitol rotunda. Many have struggled to square biblical stories like these with a post-Einstein picture of reality. But a different problem captured my attention.

I noticed the disciples' misplaced attention. While Jesus rode his cloud escalator into heaven and out of sight, the disciples kept gawking upward, craning their necks toward a vacant sky. And I noticed the angels in dazzling white, who appeared to question the disciples' heavenward gaze. "Why are you staring at the sky?" they ask, as if to say: That's not the direction you should be looking; turn your gaze back to earth, to one another, so you won't miss the miracle your lives are about to become. As if to say: *Here* is where the action is now, where the God-stuff is going on. As if they knew God was not "up," even before Copernicus did.

Five days later, I worry that Mary Clare won't be able to use her binoculars, but she's eager. We won't be like the disciples, only leering at the sky, because, along with my mission to teach her to birdwatch, she has her own: to find acorns, which means we'll be looking down, too. I've made her wear a pink hoodie over her sleeveless polka-dot dress because at 6:40 in the evening the sun will be setting, leaving us in the cool shade. It's been raining, but the front has passed, the sky is clear, the humidity is low, and everything sparkles brilliantly.

We look across the meadow and right away see an indigo bunting singing in the top of a tree, almost purple in the sun's orange light. I help Mary Clare aim and focus her binoculars, prepared for her frustration at not being able to get the bird in view, but I can tell she quickly has it in sight, as delight spreads across her face.

Then we walk toward the Oak Forest trail. I've never walked this one, but I'm guessing, given the name, it holds the most potential for finding acorns. Two black-capped chickadees buzz past and into low bushes about twenty feet ahead. I point them out to Mary Clare, and we both spot them through our binoculars. For a second, we see them hover in the air like hummingbirds, picking insects off the underside of leaves, and I follow them as they dart across the path and disappear among the trees; tracking flying birds with binoculars exceeds the skills of my neophyte companion.

A hawk flaps across the path in front of us, bursts from the trees and disappears again, a rodent clenched in its talons.

The oak leaves on the path tell us we've come the right way, and soon we hit the acorn jackpot. Mary Clare pockets several of various sizes and conditions, all dirty from lying here so long. Apparently, there are too few squirrels in this oak forest to gather all the acorns in the fall, leaving some for little girls in the spring.

On our way to the playground, I point out the indigo bunting again and comment on how it appears less brilliant now that the sun is behind the trees. I help her find it again, and she watches it for a moment before saying, "It has a white mark on its chest."

"That's just a twig, sticking up in front of the bird," I say.

Then we stop looking up and go to play.

I don't wear dazzling white when I bring the kids birdwatching, but I do for them what the angels did for the disciples—help them know where to look, *how* to look. *Don't just look at the sky, look all around*, I seem to be saying to them, both out here and in life.

And given the challenge of seeing God in the world, a challenge that seems insurmountable at times, I see how desperately I need angels who can help me see where to look and how to look and what to look at, so I won't miss the miracle my own life might become.

If noticing *Deus absconditus*—the hidden God—is hard in general, it feels distinctly impossible in midlife. Studies have suggested that the fifteen years between forty and fifty-five may be life's most challenging. These are the years when children are becoming teenagers, morphing under the influence of hormones into strangers living with you under the same roof; the years when careers become stagnant, when you might teeter on the verge of either advancement or failure, or when difficult job decisions loom; the years when marriages and partnerships can become strained, or flounder on auto-pilot; the years when aging parents need care; the years when you realize you've started saving for retirement too late and don't know how you will afford college for your children; the years when many of life's great stressors converge. In the middle of it all, how do you keep your eyes open for the presence of God?

I don't have many answers, but I do have one: we don't do it alone. We need angels—dazzling white, optional. We need companions—what I've learned from the Celtic tradition to call soul friends. If soul friends are helpful as we mature into an adult faith, they become even more necessary when we enter the threshold of midlife, the uncharted territory where the joys and calamities of life collide, the latter sometimes obscuring the former. When life spreads itself out in so many directions that it's hard to know in which direction to look, we cannot go alone. We need someone who can say, "Why are you looking in that direction? Try paying attention to *this*."

I might not always know who God is—a settledness about that comes and goes—and I might be disconcertingly unaware of what I'm paying attention to when I say I'm trying to pay attention to God. Am I looking for a mist? A warm feeling? A residue, like the ones left by ghouls in *Ghostbusters*, like the shimmering path trailing a slug?

I need what Christians throughout the ages have said I need. The Celtic leader Brigid is believed to have said, "A person without a soul friend is like a body without a head." I need someone who has been through their own transitions and has not lost God, or hasn't been lost by God, and knows it. Someone who has spent more hours in prayer and silence and solitude than I have. Someone who has faced their own demons without being undone by them, and who can encourage me to face mine, but won't reject me when I flee them in fear. Someone who is neither shocked when I say I'm not sure who God is and don't know how to find God, nor surprised when God's presence flashes in my life, and I greet it with joy. Someone who can remind me that I'm just an amateur when it comes to prayer, a beginner, but who also reminds me that amateur means "one who loves."

Someone who can help me get my bearings when I find myself dizzied by the winds of midlife stress and fear and anxiety, who can help me focus the lenses of my soul, and say, "Why don't you look for a while in that direction?"

Someone I trust enough that I can respond, "Okay."

"Oh Dad, there—up there!"

Mary Clare points into the tree branches a few feet above my head. We are leaving the play area for the car. I've just finished watching an eastern bluebird pluck plump worms from the ground, an eastern phoebe snag insects from the air, and a red-shouldered hawk glide conspicuously across the sky—all while Mary Clare played, oblivious to what was going on. But now she's the one with her eyes open.

I look in the branch and see another chickadee, so cute, dressed in black and white like a miniature groom in tuxedo.

"I heard it before I saw it," she says with a smile, pleased with herself that she spied the bird before I did, that she's the one showing *me* where to look.

WALK 15

Detective of Divinity

It's eight in the morning on Memorial Day, sixty-one degrees and humid, and I wonder if by the end of my walk I will feel too hot in my blue jeans. The rest of the family is sleeping in, so I go alone to continue my re-education in attention.

But this Audubon nature reserve is not the only place I visit regularly these days to learn attention. About once a month, usually on a Thursday afternoon, I collect my laptop, books, and journals in which I scribble ideas for lectures and articles, load my briefcase, leave the seminary early, and drive to see Sister Anna. When I started seeing Sister Anna in the fall, we met in the spiritual direction room at the seminary, but these days we sit in her study at her order's Pittsburgh residence. She used to ask if I wanted water when I arrived, but now there's usually a glass waiting for me on the table between the two grandmotherly swivel chairs we sit in. Her writing desk stands beneath the window that faces the street where I park, and through which, on cloudless May days like these, the sun bathes the room in warmth. To the right of her desk, a bookcase displays books that testify to the chief influence on her approach to spirituality: Ignatius of Loyola, the sixteenth–century founder of the Jesuits, who believed we should seek to "find God in all things."

As I have learned about Ignatian spirituality from Sister Anna and my own reading, I would summarize his spiritual approach in two words: pay attention. After all, if he is right that God is in all things, then *finding* God in all things means we can't wander through life zombie-like, or constantly distracted by the barrage of sensory data bombarding us. We have to learn to pay attention with intention.

Central to what we pay attention to, according to Ignatius, is the affective dimension of our lives—our feelings. Ignatius believed that how we respond affectively to the situations of our lives and the choices set before us can indicate to us how God is leading. He said we should notice moments of spiritual consolation—experiences of peace and joy and serenity that can sneak up on us and sneak away, but sometimes tarry—because consolation indicates a movement toward God (oh, how vast an oversimplification this is). And we should notice spiritual desolation—occasions of inner turmoil and listlessness and fear—for desolation can indicate our turning away from the intention of Divine Love (another oversimplification).

Sometimes, when I'm trying to pay attention to my own life, to recall periods of peace or interpret bouts of turmoil, I ask myself what my old college philosophy professor used to ask, "Is it God or is it gas?" But I've come to trust Sister Anna, so I can relax, believing I don't have to have it all figured out. I don't need to be able to pen an airtight theological treatise on finding God in order to trust myself to her lead and look at what she points me to, when I so often want to hurry past to get to what seems to me most important.

If I mention the joy of birdwatching with Silas on Mother's Day, she'll point to that and say, in so many words, "You want to know where God is in your life? Look at that." If I tell her about the delight on Ginger's face during our Mother's Day breakfast and my own delight at the bananas and strawberries mixed with whipped cream tumbling from their mound on the waffles; or if I tell her about the peace I feel sometimes walking in the woods, and how my thoughts settle into a mindful serenity, or how peace settles on me sometimes when I'm reading a book about looking for God; or if I tell her about how the second verse of Hymn 500 took me by surprise and choked me up so that I could only mouth the words that I knew were my truest prayer—*I ask no dream, no prophet ecstasies, no sudden rending of the veil of clay, no angel visitant, no opening skies; but take the dimness of my soul away*—she will smile, and I know what that smile means: I am telling her what I need to pay attention to, where God is making God's presence known in my life.

Sometimes when I read Ignatius's own "Rules for Discernment," they seem too scientific, too precise, as though they've got God figured out, not unlike the way a field guide to birds catalogs, describes, and defines—but is not itself alive. But in the hands of someone like Sister Anna, someone in whom knowledge has morphed into wisdom through deep experience, there is a gentle, life-giving quality to this Ignatian approach, a deep helpfulness, a sense-making. *Yes,* I sometimes think in one of those surprising but welcome moments of clarity and trust, *God is in this, and wants me to know it.*

So if I tell Sister Anna next Thursday what I spy on this walk, she might see it as a metaphor about paying attention to where God shows up.

When I move around the pond and the pavilion and turn left on Spring Hollow, I pause next to the beginning of the Oak Forest trail and see what I think is a cardinal flutter into the tree just above me, a splash of red among the green—a cardinal is the only red I ever see out here. But when I spot it with my binoculars, I see that the red is starker than a cardinal's—brighter, more scarlet—and the wings are solid black, and I recognize it as a scarlet tanager. I remember the first one I ever saw, when Ginger and I were newly married and we visited the plot of land in rural Florida her family calls the farm, a place where her dad plants peas and cucumbers, and they host picnics and marshmallow roasts. I had brought along my binoculars, my *Sibley Guide*, and a pocketsize journal. When I saw a red bird there, in a tree on the edge of the clearing, I studied it and sketched it, noting the black wings and the bright red, as well as the absence of a crest—I was making *sure* it wasn't a cardinal. After it flew away, I retreated to where the family was sitting, and I flipped through the still new *Guide* until I found the bird, read the description, and made a positive identification—a beginning birdwatcher's small triumph.

And I stand here, just as delighted as I was thirteen years ago, allowing that memory to crawl out of the storehouse and into the present, to flood me with joy. And I wonder what Sister Anna might say. Perhaps that the divine presence, too, can appear out of nowhere, and if we're paying attention we might see it. And how other things can look like God, can attract us and distract us, so that paying attention matters even more.

And when the memory of joy and joy itself meet in the moment, and the heart sings like a jazz-loving mockingbird, we don't need to ask a lot of questions or get too philosophical. We just need to let the soul whisper, *I see you God—and thanks.*

— **TRAIL FIVE** —

Confronting Midlife Fears

What we're talking about is getting to know fear, becoming familiar with fear, looking it right in the eye –not as a way to solve problems, but as a complete undoing of old ways of seeing, hearing, smelling, tasting, and thinking.

–Pema Chödrön

It often seems like fear has so invaded every part of our lives that we no longer know what a life without fear would feel like.

–Henri Nouwen

The Places That Scare You

I'm leaving the middle school, thankful for the memory my visit has given me. The International Festival was today. Student-made displays about countries all over the world crammed the cafeteria. Students were dressed representing the cultures of these countries, and many of them offered food. Simeon worked hard over the past two weeks with Kelly on a display about the United Kingdom. They set up a tri-fold with faux-gilded lettering, a map of the U.K., and a picture of the queen. Simeon dressed as a "cool, teenaged Londoner" (I couldn't tell the difference from a teenaged Pittsburgher, but that says more about me than it does about the costume) and he made scones and clotted cream, with a side of strawberry jam, for sampling.

When a bite passed my lips, I was transported back to Broad Street, Oxford, England, my junior year in college, twenty years ago. I was sitting alone by a window on the second floor of a tea shop called The Soprano, umbrellas jostling past one another on the narrow sidewalk below. A half-eaten scone sat on a plate in front of me, spread with clotted cream and jam. The other half was in one hand and a book was in the other—a new translation of Augustine's *Confessions* by Henry Chadwick that rendered lines I had memorized almost unrecognizable. I was taking a break before my tutorial at Christ Church College in early Christian history. Who knew a bite of food in a middle school cafeteria could become a means of time travel?

As I leave the school, I intend to run by the church to proofread the bulletin— I'm preaching this Sunday—until I realize I have a little over an hour before I need to pick up the other kids from school, just enough time to squeeze in my first walk this June. I'm not dressed for it though, not dressed for anything really: old Docker khakis with a hole in the back where a belt loop ripped off, a fraying white dress shirt open just enough to show a hole in the collar of my undershirt, black dress socks, and my new black Crocs, this last item a great embarrassment to Simeon— "Crocs, Dad? Those are so 2010!" Tiny studs on the insoles of the Crocs grip the bottoms of my socks as I walk and, peristalsis-like, draw them into the toes of the shoes so I have to stop and pull them up every few minutes—something I'm sure neither a cool Londoner nor Pittsburgher would deign to do.

I know where I'm going, my inappropriate attire notwithstanding: to the place I always avoid, the one place that scares me.

———————

I've known all along about the risks out here from the first time I read the warning on the map that absolves the Audubon Society of any responsibility should I injure myself: "All outdoor activities involve some risk, including falling trees or branches, wet or slippery conditions, and interaction with animals and insects." By using these trails, they tell me, I am "agreeing to assume those risks and to hold harmless Audubon Society of Western Pennsylvania for the risks." I don't know the legal status of such a statement, but I take its point: I have been duly warned. Indeed, when an enormous tree fell twenty yards from me the last time I was here, smashing a bench, I thought, *Well, I shouldn't be surprised; I have been apprised of the danger.*

Other signs warn me as well. One informs me of the prevalence of ticks and the potential for contracting Lyme disease, and a sign on the bee hive announces that bees will sting when they feel threatened. I don't need a sign to warn me not to approach the geese, especially the ones today being followed by goslings that I'm sure they are more than prepared to defend. But nothing has scared me, nothing has felt unsafe except for the place I'm going now: the tree-top lookout, a rickety, wooden promontory jutting from the side of a hill and over a ravine, putting anyone brave enough to walk out to the end at eye level with the tops of trees rising from the valley below.

Which turns out to be about everyone but me.

———————

A few days ago we arrived early for Simeon's choir concert at the middle school. Ginger and Silas went in to save seats, and Mary Clare and I walked over to a nature trail nearby. The trail edged along the top of a hill that sloped precipitously toward a stream at the bottom of the valley. Mary Clare walked ahead of me, in a hurry, but close enough that I could still hear her jabbering.

"I want to be a scientist when I grow up, a scientist and a book writer—a scientist and a book writer and a painter." I told her that was possible, that she could paint and write about what she studies, as I tried to catch up, keep her close.

"Remember that bird book by David Sibley? He studies birds, writes books about birdwatching, and paints birds to help people identify them."

The path narrowed across a stream that spilled down the hill, feeding the stream below. We had to step across on flat, slippery stones, and I grasped Mary Clare's hand, interposing my body between her and the hill. Across the stream, the path continued to narrow and sneaked closer to the edge. I pushed Mary Clare away from the edge, even though she wanted to look down, and kept crowding her over with my body. But I couldn't fool her. My pretensions at keeping her safe couldn't mask the deeper cause of my behavior: I was afraid—not just for her, but for myself.

"Dad, if you are going to be a scientist with me, you have to face your fears."

I remember her admonition as I climb a muddy slope on Spring Hollow in these less-than-ideal shoes, and ruminate on the way fear, as long as I can remember, has narrowed my path through life, sometimes obstructing it, and frequently determining which way I would go. I realize that I don't want my fears and aversions and anxieties—and the dangerous cocktail they make when mixed—to chart the next forty years of my life. I wonder if a brief attempt at facing one fear, my fear of heights, might create an opening for me to address others. So I make for the tree-top lookout, and when I arrive, I sit down on the bench, where I usually wait while the kids dash out to the end of the lookout and Ginger follows calmly behind, and I pull up my socks.

Then I stand. Turn. Breathe. Step forward.

When I turned forty, no posted placards announced the risks, or warned me what I should watch out for, what I should fear. But I don't need them. I only have to settle myself for a few moments, let the fog of activity and distraction evaporate, and I can read the warning signs on my own soul, see my own versions of the midlife fears that afflict so many.

I'm afraid of running out of money—not tomorrow, not next month—but afraid of not having enough to put my kids through college, to help them make it through like I did, without having to work or take out loans that will burden them for years. I'm afraid of not having enough to retire well, to move into a nice community that tends the lawn and repairs the roof so I can focus on traveling to, say, Oxford, and can sit in a tea room with my wife and tell her stories of when I was here forty-five years earlier. I'm afraid of our becoming that couple in political ads, trying to convince you the other party's economic plan will spell ruin, the couple that sits wordlessly at their kitchen table, brows creased with worry, a calculator and a notepad and a pile of bills staring up at them.

I'm afraid I won't achieve my dreams; they keep changing, anyway. I'm afraid I won't get recognized. Already I know I'll never play the Phantom of the Opera on Broadway, likely not even in community theater. But I'm running out of time to develop an expertise and get noticed, to become known for something, *anything*. I sometimes fantasize about going back to school and earning another degree—a

Master of Fine Arts in creative writing. I do the calculation. What do they say—ten thousand hours of intentional practice to become an expert at something? Perhaps in a few years, if I'm devoted, I could be a well-regarded essayist, winning a six-figure advance on a book and landing an endowed chair in creative writing at a university that offers tuition remission for the children of employees, thus addressing fear number one at the same time.

I'm afraid of losing my memory.

I'm afraid that the rare rheumatoid arthritis I've lived with for twenty years will fuse my spine or initiate a string of hip, shoulder, and neck surgeries.

I'm afraid I'll never publish another book.

I'm afraid my anxieties will close in on me and cut me off from real living.

I'm afraid the changes in my faith might not end where I hope, that my oscillating between trust and doubt will get stuck in the "doubt" position, and never swing back. How easy it is sometimes to talk of God and Jesus and Divine Love, and believe it all—to want to get lost in an ocean of Love! Then the suspicion comes that everything I see is an accident, a fluke realization of the most miniscule of possibilities, that anything like "meaning" is an imposition, a figment of our imaginations. (But how could a choir of sixth-graders making beautiful music together be an accident?) When you earn a living writing, speaking, preaching, and teaching about God, losing faith has tangible consequences, like ending up as a funeral director or a mindfulness instructor.

I'm afraid I will become what I know I can't avoid: an unfinished symphony. Priest and spiritual writer Ronald Rolheiser writes, "In all of our lives, there is a huge gap between what our hearts demand and what we can actually attain in this life. Consequently we are frustrated, never able to attain the finished symphony." Will I ever know what my life as finished symphony might sound like?

Who, walking through the wilderness of midlife, hasn't sensed fears around security, meaning, accomplishment, faith—fears that stalk the edges of awareness like revenants? But I also believe, with the monks of old, that naming our fears robs them of power, makes them less daunting to face.

The plaque nailed to a wooden railing says this tree-top lookout was built in 1986 in memory of someone. That the lookout is thirty years old does not inspire my confidence. Neither does the joint in the railing secured by a new silver bracket and screws, new hardware that highlights the nearby rusted screws, coming loose.

I can't look into all of my midlife fears today—that's the work of half-a-lifetime, for sure. It will be hard enough to determine which ones need to be accepted as they are, which need to be actively resisted, and which can be ignored. But maybe I can get a start here, practice a new response, build confidence going forward.

I grab the handrail and slowly walk out. With each step the ground slopes further away, and the narrow wooden legs supporting the structure lengthen and, to my mind, get wobblier. At the end of the boardwalk is an octagonal platform, with waist-high railings on seven sides, affording a nearly 360-degree view of the valley and the hills on the other side. I can't go out to the end yet, not all the way, but I walk onto the platform and turn to the right railing. I guess I'm twenty-five yards off the ground. A maple tree stands inches from the railing, close enough that I could reach out and touch its trunk—if I weren't afraid.

I stand six inches back, place both hands on the railing, and look ahead into leafy branches in the distance—maple, oak, others I can't identify. I can see the ground out of my peripheral vision and begin to feel like I'm going to float out and forward, like there's a gravitational force that wants to draw me not down—at least not yet—but forward, through the railing and out over the ground. My grip tightens; my arms tense.

I tilt my head downward, and I see the ground through the slats in the railing. My head starts to feel full, dizzy, and my legs weaken from the knees down, a tingling sensation beginning behind my knees and then curving around to the front, then on down. So I revert to my forward gaze.

The next time I look down I try to do what I learned in a mindfulness class years ago: I give my attention to my body, let the physical sensations of fear fill my awareness, without trying to change anything. I feel the tingling in my legs, the lightness in my head; I feel my breath become shallow, my heart rate quicken, my grip tighten on the railing. *Let your attention rest on your body*, I can hear the instructor saying, *releasing the fearful thoughts that accompany the experience*. And I do.

For about thirty seconds, before I count the experiment a success.

I faced a fear, felt it. That's good enough for one day. The goal wasn't to conquer it. How many fears, after all, are susceptible to being conquered? I have the rest of my life to tackle the others.

WALK 17

Stop Riding the Brakes on the Heart

Ignatius of Loyola taught a way to read Scripture by putting ourselves right in the story. He said that we can enter the story of God through our imaginations, using all of our senses. We can ask what we see, hear, feel, smell, taste as we sit on the grass eating the bread Jesus has multiplied, for instance, or warm our hands over the fire as the authorities interrogate our friend Jesus, or stumble down the mountain after seeing Jesus transfigured. We can even, Ignatius said, have imaginative conversations with characters in the story—with Jesus. This, he said, is prayer.

When I teach about this imaginative reading of Scripture, I often use for illustration Rembrandt's painting *The Storm on the Sea of Galilee*, painted in 1633 when he was twenty-seven years old. In it, foamy waves lift and flood a boat that lists toward the shadowy side of the painting. The passengers frantically secure rope, pull oars, and lower sails. One appears to be praying, another vomiting over the side. A sleepy Jesus, face aglow, has just been awakened.

If you count the number of figures in the boat, you'll find one more than you'd expect: not thirteen—twelve disciples plus Jesus—but fourteen. That's because Rembrandt painted himself into the scene, his likeness staring at the viewer, one hand clasping a rope, the other securing a hat on his head, a look of panic across his face. Rembrandt did what Ignatius recommended: he entered the story and experienced the scene in all its chaos and fear.

There's no way to know whether it was prayer for him, but it has been for me over the last several months, as I've been working with Sister Anna through what Ignatius called the Spiritual Exercises—a plan for meditating on the life of Christ in order to discern the presence and guidance of the Spirit in my life. Sometimes it's been great, and sometimes hard; sometimes revelatory, and sometimes tedious—and almost always too early in the morning.

And sometimes surprising, like when I found myself in the boat, yelling at Jesus to wake up. "Why have you been asleep lately? Don't you know my life feels like this storm sometimes? Don't you know I'm afraid?"

Sharing that prayer experience with Sister Anna began a conversation about what I'm afraid of, including not only flying and driving through the mountains, but also the other fears I've mentioned: going broke, losing faith, hearing the symphony of my life decrescendo into nothingness. Fortunately, she didn't take her cue from popular faith-guides and say, "Just believe! Just have faith!" Instead, she said something I'd not thought consciously, but believe I already knew.

"You can pray this way with your life, too, not just Scripture. You can take one of those fears and enter it contemplatively, enter the story of your fear. You can explore it, experience it in your imagination, look for Christ there, wake him up if you have to; you can pray through your fears this way."

And maybe emerge on the other side? I thought as she spoke.

I also realized that I don't just have to do this in my imagination, because I know a place that scares me, and I can walk there, study my fear, and go home changed—stronger—even if still afraid.

To the tree-top lookout I venture once more, a little further out this time, to enter my fear again and, if I'm lucky, to see beyond it—a warm-up for the rest of midlife.

"Have they cleared the tree that fell last month?" I ask Scott, the birdwatching guide who chatted too much for Silas last year. I'm wondering if I'll be able to get past, or if I should take a different route.

"The tree was so large and penetrated so far into the ground when it fell, I had to hire a chainsaw master to show me and the other guys how to cut it up."

When I pass the remains of the fallen tree, I see what he meant. The larger branches look like they'd buried themselves a couple of feet when they fell. What remains of one branch that impaled the ground now looks like a stump in the middle of the trail.

As I mosey though the valley, enjoying a day of low-humidity with the temperature in the mid-seventies, I notice how dense and green the brush has grown by this second week of summer. The weeds are so much higher; the walls of green on each side of me appear impenetrable.

I glance up from the valley and see my destination high above.

And I remember Mary Clare. Two weeks ago, she had her first swim meet. She'd talked all day about being nervous, and during warm-up laps the tears started as she swam, increasing the salt content of the pool. After she got out she cried in her mother's arms. A few minutes earlier, I had seen her coach giving her a pep-talk. When her race was announced, she dropped into the water, still wiping her eyes, though ready to start when her teammate reached her end. As her teammate finished her lap and touched the side, Mary Clare pushed off, gained on her opponent in the next lane, and finished with a flourish. She climbed out of the pool, and we hugged and cheered.

As she walked with me to the car to get a book I could read until her next race, I said, "I'm proud of you. Do you know why?"

"Because I faced my fears?"

"Yes," I said, "just like you told me to do, remember?"

"Are you still afraid of high places?" she asked.

"Maybe, but I'm not going to let that keep me from doing the things I want to do."

Now, as I climb the last hill, the ground dry and cracked from a week without rain, I'm thankful that the daughter has become the teacher.

I don't pause to look at the dedication plaque or investigate the rusting brackets or contemplate the structure's age. Instead, I walk slowly out to the end, to the farthest point, supported by my staff. I think, *There is a view I will miss if I don't walk out*. One thing I'm learning is that it's okay to miss things; we can't see it all because of the limits of bodies and time and space. On the other hand, opportunities present themselves. Some might even say, as I would at times, God invites us to new possibilities, new experiences that will challenge us, change us, teach us. But I know all too well that the closed doors of fear can stand in the way, like a fallen tree obstructing a path.

I imagine the boardwalk out to the platform as the threshold of midlife, with all its fears and risks. I don't know if there's a way not to cross it, not to venture out, but I'm sure you could do it with head down and eyes close, keeping your eyes fixed firmly on the familiar, the safe. But the afternoon of life awaits with wider vistas and deeper valleys and nearly limitless horizons, and what a shame it would be to miss them because you are afraid.

I pause and remember the words of former Harvard Divinity School dean Samuel Miller:

> We fear failure more than we love life, so we refuse the great ventures. . . . Stop riding the brakes on the heart. The soul will never grow, tied down in bed with the shades drawn. The higher and more secure we build the barricades of care and caution to protect ourselves, the deeper grows the grave we call life.

I don't know if this experiment indicates faith in God, or bravery, or mere silliness, but it's something I have to do. It's practice, a little bit of fear-facing now so that I might do it better when it matters most.

I get close enough to the railing at the end to reach out and grab it without having to lean forward. And the view *is* breathtaking. The valley slopes away, falls into a deep ravine, the lowest point of which I cannot see. To my left and right the leaf-covered ground seems close, but ahead of me the earth plunges. I know where it goes—I've walked around down there—but from here it seems not to stop. The black oak to my left has been looking out from this spot for decades without faltering or running away, as has the maple tree to my right. I want to learn from them, learn to be steady, solid, resolute in the face of fear.

What I'm really looking at is the rest of my life: its slopes, down which I could fall; its heights, which, with effort, I might reach; its blessed, frightening finitude—an end I cannot see but toward which I journey; and its company, like these trees, reminding me I don't cross this threshold or face my fears alone.

— TRAIL SIX —

Raising Vocational Questions

What many Christians are missing in their lives is a sense of vocation. The word itself means a call or summons, so that having a vocation means more than having a job. It means answering a specific call; it means doing what one is meant to do.

–Barbara Brown Taylor

Vocation does not come from willfulness. It comes from listening. I must listen to my life and try to understand what it is truly about– quite apart from what I would like it to be about–or my life will never represent anything real in the world, no matter how earnest my intentions.

–Parker Palmer

WALK 18

Acorn or Switchback?

The Scripture passage for my morning meditation a few days ago: the story of Jesus's healing of the blind man at Bethsaida—his one intervention that required a follow-up. Adopting an alternative therapy approach, Jesus spits in his hands and presses them to the blind man's eyes. Upon this first application, the man regains some sight. "I can see people, but they look like trees walking," he says, a line I can't read without thinking of J. R. R. Tolkien's talking, walking trees, the Ents, in *The Lord of the Rings*, or Macbeth as he watches Birnam wood come to Dunsinane.

Jesus tries again, and, after this second attempt, the man sees clearly.

The episode serves as a hinge in Mark's gospel as the story makes its inevitable turn toward Jerusalem and the Cross. In the chapters that follow this healing, Jesus teaches his disciples about true servanthood, but like the blind man, the disciples don't get it on the first try. And they don't get it on the second, or third. Until they encounter the risen Jesus, their vision remains blurred.

On the morning I read this passage, I wasn't thinking about physical healings or Jesus's teaching about discipleship. I was thinking how midlife can be a kind of hinge, as well, how, at midlife, life's door inches open, and, when we peer through the crack to the other side, we might gain, if not clarity, at least a new perspective on old struggles.

For me, what has seemed murky has been my vocation. I've absorbed so much vocational wisdom that says I need to find my one passion, my single area of giftedness, that my failure over forty years to find my One Big Thing has led to a frustrating, cloudy, and sometimes unsatisfying sense of vocation. But perhaps I've been looking for the wrong thing, asking the wrong questions. I'm wondering if midlife can be a chance for questions of vocation to surface again in a new context, with new questions; maybe this time the murkiness will give way to a settled clarity. Then again, maybe not.

"What are you thinking about on your walks this July?" Silas asks. We are in the car on the way to Beechwood Farms at seven in the evening. The others have gone to the neighborhood pool, but Silas gets bored at the pool, so he chose to come with me. He's also interested in my forty-walks project and the book I'm writing about it.

"I've got vocation on my mind these days," I say.

"What's vocation?"

I struggle to find words to make a concept that I'm still wrestling with intelligible to an eleven-year-old. "Vocation is what you do with your life," I say. "It can be related to your job or career, but it's also connected to the meaning and purpose of your life."

"So is this the first book you're writing that's not about God?"

"Actually," I say, "vocation comes from the Latin word *vocare*, which means 'to call,' so it can refer to the work—or way of life—God calls you to." As I say this, I think about how, at seventeen, I gave up my long-standing dream to sing on Broadway when I sensed God calling me to be a preacher. Now I'm a seminary professor—a work to which I felt a sense of call—who sometimes preaches resuscitated sermons when I'm invited. And, even now, I sense my call shifting, widening. It's happened so much that I'm not sure what it even means to say I have *a* calling.

"Some people know their vocation early in life," I continue, thinking aloud, "and it remains strong and consistent throughout their lives. But for others"—I slip into autobiography here—"it can take a long time to become clear, if it ever does. Look at me: am I a pastor, preacher, or a professor? And lately I've wanted to give more of myself to writing." Silas knows I want to write a children's novel, but I can't imagine how that could possibly relate to my vocation.

As I speak, a flash of memory: Mary Clare on the Oak Forest trail a few weeks ago, stuffing as many acorns into her pocket as would fit, and I realize vocation is often thought of as an acorn.

"Let's call it the acorn theory of vocation," I venture, curious to see if the child next to me is still listening. He appears to be, so I continue. "The acorn already has the DNA to become an oak—its future is written in the double helixes of its genome. Under the right conditions—when it gets water, light, and nourishment, the right amount at the right times—it will grow into an oak tree. Many people think vocation is like that. Each person has what they are meant to do already inside of them at an early age, they just have to discover it, hope that under the right conditions it reveals itself and grows into their vocation."

I've been operating under this theory for a very long time. Even as my work has changed, I have continued to chase my one true vocation. I've heard Frederick Buechner's definition of vocation so many times—"The place God calls you to is the place where your deep gladness and the world's deep hunger meet"—that I can become frantic searching for that place.

How many nights have I sat reading Parker Palmer's *Let Your Life Speak: Listening to the Voice of Vocation*, hoping his Quaker wisdom might spark a realization? I know Ginger would get nervous whenever she saw me reading it, a clear sign that the tectonic plates of my vocation were slipping. I remember one night, several years ago, I was already in bed reading, propped up by a tan study-buddy, the slim pink volume in my hand. I was reading Palmer's suggestion to look for clues to your vocation in your childhood interests, passions, and proclivities. In these childhood memories, he suggests, you might find strands of your vocational DNA. Ginger walked in to get ready for bed, and when she saw the book, a look of worry flashed across her face. She needn't have worried, however, because, when I looked back at my elementary years, I saw little more than my passion for lying on my parents' bed, watching *He-Man and the Masters of the Universe* and eating junk food. In neither of these proclivities could I glean portents of a calling.

"Here I am at forty," I say to Silas, concluding what has become an uninspiring oration, "and I still don't know what I want to be when I grow up."

Cars crowd the parking lot. A woman hurrying toward the education building tells us there's a free talk on timberwolves. Silas flashes me a *don't even think about it* look, and we head toward Pine Hollow, which the map describes as "the longest and most rigorous trail." I've got the right companion.

To get to Pine Hollow we have to trek along Spring Hollow a while, then dash across Vista to Meadowview, a trail flanked by walls of green as tall as I am. Silas can see how the trail narrows, so he hikes up his over-the-calf shamrock socks to protect himself from any encroaching poison ivy; we've seen plenty already. He is chattier than usual, perhaps making up for having to listen to me in the car. Even though Silas walks behind me, he continues to quiz me, questions tumbling out of him like coins from a winning slot machine:

What movies are you looking forward to?

What children's books do you think they should make into movies?

What are you excited about coming up this summer?

What are you looking forward to on our trip to Chicago?

What do you think I should look forward to in Chicago?

I answer his questions as best I can, interspersing my assessment of the trail, which most often goes like this: "I don't recognize anything—it's so overgrown; the first time I was here must have been before the spring monsoons."

The trail angles steeply downhill, leading us into the deepest ravine at the nature reserve. When we cross the same creek a second time I feel disoriented, though the rocky slopes and a small waterfall look vaguely familiar. The trail presents a series of small, sharp curves, not visible on the map, leading into a gorge, and then up and out. We pass a sign I don't remember. "No horses or vehicles," it reads, and I can't conceive how either could get down here. As we begin our assent, a makeshift staircase—slats of wood embedded in the side of the hill—gives us a foothold, as well as prevents the side of the hill from eroding, I suspect. We arrive at the pine part of the hollow, and I say again how I don't recognize where we are; there are so many more needles on the ground, obscuring the path. I'm huffing up the hill.

"This *is* rigorous," I say breathlessly.

"I wouldn't say that," my spry sidekick responds.

At one point we are facing west, looking at the setting sun through the pines, which means our backs are toward the main buildings, but inspecting the map, I can't find a single place on this trail where such an orientation would be possible. I'm not sure where we are, but when I hear the sirens from a nearby volunteer fire station and the rumble of car tires on a road, I can make a pretty good guess. After a third creek-crossing, clearly delineated on the map, we can pinpoint our location and discover: it's still a long way back.

———

Meandering, confused, disoriented—that's what *we've* been on the trail. Our experience, I realize, provides an alternative metaphor for vocation to the acorn. I've been asking the question, What's my one true vocation? I've scanned my childhood memories and my Myers-Briggs type and my Enneagram profile for clues. I've looked at my many gladnesses for my *deep* gladness, but they seem to have changed depths in different stages of my life, so that I haven't even gotten around to considering the world's deep need. And I still wonder, what is my One True Vocation?

But maybe vocation is more like walking a narrow trail: too many switchbacks to see very far ahead, with some places of beauty along the way; places, too, where progress is made effortlessly, as well as others where it's difficult simply to get a footing; spots where you wonder, *How could I be facing this way?*, and others where you think, *I know exactly where I am*; some signs that confuse, and others that help you find your bearings. Maybe that's what vocation is like for some of us. Maybe getting used to the uncertainty, even allowing it; ceasing to resist—maybe that's the work of vocation as the hinge swings open the door to the second half of life.

By this metaphor, I can't be sure what the next turn will bring, but I can give myself fully to what I'm doing now, what I feel momentarily bold enough to name as *calling* now, give myself to *this* gladness, *this* work before me, while acknowledging that other shifts might occur—in fact, are beginning. Still, even if I stop hunting for my One True Vocation, that doesn't mean I'll reject it should it appear.

WALK 19

The Weasel in All of Us?

I've not seen a weasel on my walks, as far as I know, though I have seen plenty of other animals. I'm walking beside a rough-hewn fence on my way to the Oak Forest trail, watching a squirrel—that might resemble a weasel?—atop the fence. The squirrel sees me and scampers along at my pace, its tail waving and lashing with each undulation of its body. I can just hear the scratch of its claws on the wood. It stays several feet in front of me, pausing to peer back on occasion.

"I'm following you," I say, but he doesn't respond, just keeps moving.

And the song sparrows—certainly no relation to the weasel—are plentiful, their melodies all around me. One on a thistle stalk in the meadow lifts its beak toward the sky like the lead singer of a praise band, throwing his notes heavenward. I can see clearly the larger brown spot in the center of his speckled breast. And this groundhog, it swaggers across the path in front of me and disappears into the thistle, waddling his way to the pond across the meadow. When I look up from the ground-hog, the squirrel is gone; I've lost him, the little weasel. I would make a horrible spy.

Squirrels, chipmunks, birds, bunnies—but no weasels. Yet it was a weasel Annie Dillard observed that prompted her to articulate what I now call the weasel theory of vocation, a close cousin to the acorn theory. Dillard, who *would* make a great spy, watched a weasel, locked eyes with it, and then spent the next week contemplating the animal. That weasel, she wrote, can teach us how to live—the weasel, so naturally himself, who couldn't be other than the small predator he is, who marches to instinct's drum.

"The weasel lives by necessity and we live by choice, hating necessity and dying at last ignobly in its talons. I would like to live as I should, as the weasel lives as he should." Vocation, for Dillard, is living as we *should*. It's not avoiding the one calling—the pattern of living and working and playing and dying that is ours—but abandoning ourselves to its necessity. Because we don't have access to instinct in the same way as a weasel, clouded as our apprehension is by our own willfulness, we have to search for that vocation. "The thing is to stalk your calling in a certain skilled and supple way, to locate the most tender and live spot and plug into that pulse." She calls this work grasping "your one necessity."

The groundhog follows his necessity to water. The squirrel obeys the necessity of self-preservation and avoids me. The song sparrow tosses tunes into the air as necessity has taught him. They are all weasels in their own way. But I know this much about myself by now: I am not a weasel, if being a weasel means knowing your *one* necessity. And I'm becoming increasingly comfortable, or at least increasingly intermittently comfortable, with the idea that I am a dabbling, dilettantish, sometimes frumpy, scattered middle-aged man, whose only necessity seems to be being distracted by the many possible necessities vying for his attention at any given time. This condition used to drive me crazy, lead to inner monologues of self-recrimination and comparison to others who, like Dillard, *have* found their one necessity. *No, I'm okay with this situation*, I tell myself, try to convince myself.

Today, though, a different question bothers me as I ponder Frederick Buechner's definition: "The place God calls you to is the place where your deep gladness and the world's deep hunger meet." Today the second half trips me up.

Does my vocation—my peculiar blend of interests and gladnesses and modest competencies that comprise my contribution to the world; my teaching and preaching, and loving and raising kids, and washing dishes; my hammering out a clunky book review, as I did this morning for an academic journal that maybe forty people will read, because writing such things is expected in my profession; my scribbling about faith and doubt and the weather on these walks and the random thoughts I think between them—does my vocation, does any of what I do, even come close to touching *the world's deep need?*

I'm sure it's a question artists sometimes ask, those people who have stalked their vocations and given themselves over to the necessity of beauty—like Annie Dillard, who can't not observe the world and her life in it then lay down sentence after sentence like a bricklayer laying brick.

Or like the master potter I had tea with last week in Minnesota, Richard Bresnahan. One of his apprentices heated the tea over an open fire in the center of the studio, while Bresnahan sat at a potter's wheel, his hands fashioning local Minnesota clay. When the tea was ready, the apprentice handed me a small Japanese-looking cup. Bresnahan apprenticed in Japan for several years in the 1970s, before setting up a studio on the campus of St. John's University in Collegeville, Minnesota, where he's made his art for the past thirty-seven years with single-minded devotion. I sat, my hands cradling the cup, its heat causing gentle pain in my palms. Bresnahan paused from his work and joined us, but he didn't pause for long. The kiln, which Bresnahan constructed in 1994, is fired once a year and takes seven weeks to load because Bresnahan's studio produces almost six thousand pieces of pottery a year, and *over four thousand of them are his.*

After tea, I followed an apprentice into the gift shop and asked his opinion about what to buy. He spotted an elegant, spiral cup, brown with copper and maroon swirls up the sides. When he looked at the bottom and saw Bresnahan's signature, he said, "Oh, I'm surprised this is still here. You should buy this—definitely buy this."

Annie Dillard puts hundreds of words on a page. Richard Bresnahan puts thousands of pots in a kiln. Do either of them ever wonder, *Am I touching the world's deep need*?

Does the world need more words and pots?

Am *I* touching the world's deep need? I ask that question sometimes, though I wouldn't dare call myself an artist or claim to engender beauty in the world, and feel sheepish even now thinking about myself after considering these masters. They have each found their one star and they follow it determinedly. My vocation seems more like a constellation—many stars in a sometimes-discernable pattern, some burning more brightly at different times of my life. Lately, the star that has been burning brightest, the one I can't not pay attention to, is the longing to write. As the hinge on the door of my vocation swings a little wider, I peer into a room of stories seeking expression, waiting to be told.

I know why. When I want to read, I seek books, stories, essays that will make me laugh and cry, that will touch me, that will make me *feel*. And when I feel, it reminds me I'm alive and awake, and those feelings—the sadness that rests in the bend of my right elbow, the laughter that aggravates the arthritis in my sternum—become hinges themselves, opening the doors that allow me to notice the movement of divine Love in my life. The vocational longing I've noticed lately, and am finally heeding, is simple: I want to do that for others. This work seems to be saying it wants more of me—not all of me, but more of my time and effort, more of my attention.

What would Buechner say? Does the world need my stories, my reflections that may or may not offer insight? Does it need my scribbling any more than it needs my teaching, or needed my preaching, or my singing in days long ago? Is there a deep need in the world that my ramblings about squirrels scampering along fences can touch? If we took an opinion poll, I'm afraid I know what the answer would be—no. Not when the climate is changing and the poor are becoming poorer and racism is rebounding and human trafficking flourishes. What are my words in the face of these challenges, these needs?

Then I remember Dorothy Day, the twentieth-century writer, activist, pacifist, and founder of the Catholic Worker Movement, who was devoted to offering unqualified hospitality to the poor in a way that had God's fingerprints all over it. She had a favorite quote from her favorite author, Dostoyevsky: "The world will be saved by beauty." Could that mean that we too often think of what the world needs in narrow, utilitarian, calculable ways? Beauty reminds us that what the world needs can't always be measured, weighed, and parceled out into the blinking rectangles of an Excel spreadsheet. Maybe there are deep soul needs, spirit needs—the need to laugh and cry and dance, the need to connect with other human beings at a level more profound than the merely transactional—needs that are touched by beauty, broadly conceived: aesthetic beauty, of course, and moral beauty, that beauty of simple kindness; mathematical and scientific beauty—the beauty of an equation or a theorem, of an astronomer at the telescope; the beauty of the poet with her paper; the beauty of the potter at his wheel fashioning a cup—a cup I can hold and sip, a cup I can buy and give to my wife in a couple of weeks for our fourteenth anniversary and watch her hold tenderly in her own cupped hands. All of this is beauty— life-saving, even.

And maybe it's beauty understood broadly enough to encompass the meager marks I'm making on this page that try to tell the story of a soul wondering who he is and why he's here and how he can see more clearly the beauty of the Love that called him into being, so that someone else might read them, cup their own hands around the stories, feel some warmth, and be reminded they are alive and that they matter. Might that be one small thing the world needs right now?

I'm standing in the rain at the edge of the pond, holding my umbrella. It's been humid the whole walk, and my t-shirt clings to my torso. A dozen goldfish are kissing the surface of the water. I step closer and a frog leaps in, scattering the crowd of fish. The goldfish are goldfishing; the frog, frogging. Somewhere the squirrel is squirreling, and the song sparrow is sparrowing. Somewhere else, I feel it: a Dillard is Dillarding, and a potter is pottering.

And me? I'm Rogering: taking a walk, scribbling a few notes, standing in the rain, considering the meaning of it all, after which I will drop some books off at the library, buy a couple memoirs on the sale rack I'm likely never to read, and then turn my notes into some paragraphs on vocation, not worrying—yet—whether they might be what the world needs.

Meanwhile, a weasel is weaseling, saying yes to the dictates of instinct and necessity, leaving the choice of how to live beautifully to non-weasels like me.

— TRAIL SEVEN —

Hearing the Sounds of Silence

*Just as there are two nights, there are two silences,
one is frightening and the other is peaceful.*

–Henri Nouwen

*Silence is an urgent necessity for us;
silence is necessary if we are to hear God
speaking in eternal silence;
our own silence is necessary if God is to hear us.*

–Martin Laird

WALK 20

The Canvas of Silence

On my way to walk, I dropped the kids off at the church for Vacation Bible School, that weeklong extravaganza of noise, costume, song, and movement designed to keep kids interested long enough to imbibe the basic certainties of the Christian faith. Simeon and Mary Clare came enthusiastically; Silas, with his allergy to campiness, not so much.

I stuck around long enough to hear the beginning of the music session: jazzed-up kids on a large-screen TV, encouraging the youngsters in the sanctuary to move, clap, and sing along to the music blaring through the sound system.

"He is the light," the children sang in unison, except for my unenthused son. "He breaks through the darkness. Jesus will guide through every dark time." With that, I could guess the theme of the day. At such volume, it would have been hard to miss.

Now I do what I realize has become a routine: I walk from my car to the meadow of thistle. I stand at the wooden fence bordering the meadow and I look out across it, toward the pond and the surrounding trees, and take in what goes on in and around the meadow. Sometimes I see thistle jostled by a groundhog trekking to the pond, or song sparrows flitting from stalk to stalk or rustling near the ground. Sometimes I see a red-shouldered hawk wing his way from one side to another before vanishing among branches. Today I notice the sun, two-thirds of the way behind the trees, backlighting two cedar waxwings perched high in a tree, silhouetting their crested forms. I watch as they leap from the branches, catch insects midair, and flutter back, displaying their characteristic movement.

My feet stand shoulder width apart, my hands rest on the splintery fence rail, and my mind calms, as if it's relinquishing its concerns and flying to join the birds and the meadow and the sky. I didn't know how badly I needed this—the silence—after a family vacation visiting friends outside of Chicago. Eleven humans and one dog lived in a sixteen-hundred-square-foot house for four days. We spent one morning downtown dodging traffic, buying chocolate, and wandering, imprisoned, in the American Girl Doll store. Yesterday we endured eight hours in the van, with bickering in the backseat, the blasting of the Broadway cast recording of *Wicked*, and the constant buzz of road noise. And then the Vacation Bible School cacophony twenty minutes ago. All of that—it sloughs off me like the dead skin of a snake, and I enter the soothing sounds, the conspicuous silence of nature.

On Goldenrod, near the pond, a yellow and black butterfly wafts on the wind, silent wings propelling it this way and that. I try to sketch the shape, teardrops dangling from the wings, so I might identify it later—some kind of swallowtail—but what I sketch looks more like a tooth on the sign at a dentist's office than a butterfly. I find I'm jealous of the butterfly, of its silent, easy freedom.

I turn onto Violet. I listen to the sounds as I negotiate the uneven path: traffic rumbling down Harts Run Road, tires crunching loose gravel; the screaming sirens of an emergency vehicle; titmice and chickadees chirping their warning cry, indicating a hawk nearby; a blue jay shouting its alarm as well, confirming a predator's proximity; the stream gurgling; and cicadas throbbing eerily, their sound swelling and diminishing like ocean waves rolling ashore.

I look up and see stealthy evening light poking through the interstices of leaves above.

This is not total silence; I can hear distinct, identifiable noises. The experience differs from life among the throng of day-to-day sounds that all meld into one continual background noise—the white noise that erases the integrity of each sound. Here, the noises arise out of the silence; they can be heard and identified against its wide and spacious backdrop. Silence forms the canvas on which the color of each sound appears. Nature wields the brush, and each stroke is unique in hue and texture and length against the silence, the ground of its very possibility. I can still see the bright white silence around the edges, and in between, as if the silence itself were presenting each noise as a gift, a gesture of welcome.

How different from the racket in a house with eleven people, from the din of traffic and human bustle of Chicago, from the feigned enthusiasm and raucous energy of a Vacation Bible School.

A gesture, a gift: rest here in the silence between, the silence surrounding, the silence grounding the possible.

"I disagree with the premise of this chapter, that everyone needs more silence," the man sitting next to me said.

A couple of weeks ago I met for breakfast with a men's group from a large church nearby, a favor for a friend of mine. Also, they were reading my book, and it's hard to say no to folks who have bought and are discussing your book, even if they meet at six in the morning at a greasy dive with a waitress who calls all the men, old and young alike, "honey."

We sat in a private dining room that could have accommodated three times our number, and I would have been happy for three times our number to have bought my book. There were eight, which was probably more people discussing my book than anywhere else that morning. It didn't take long for me to realize many of these men were "we've-got-to-take-back-our-country-for-God" kind of Christians, and I began to worry how they would react to my spirituality, given its more "learn-to-let-go-of-everything-including-our-country" character. For the most part they were pleasant and appreciative, except for the fellow sitting to my right, the man who voiced his concern about the chapter on silence while he shoveled his brown sugar-sweetened, berry-laden oatmeal into his mouth.

"I don't need silence," he said. "I have too much silence. I'm a middle-aged, divorced man. I live alone. I have all the silence I need, more than I need."

It was too early for an argument—I'd only had one cup of coffee—so I nodded and said, "I see." But what I thought was, *You don't fool me. You don't have silence. You have a radio buzzing, or a television blaring, or earbuds jammed in your ears, while you pace around your apartment or log steps on your treadmill. You do anything to distract yourself from the silence, so you don't have to hear the noises within you: the creaking ache of loneliness; the inner monologue in which you call yourself a failure, blame yourself for your divorce; the video loop in your mind that replays the argument you had the last time you saw your twenty-year-old son and told him you didn't understand him and never had. You'll do anything to run from that silence.*

I wasn't being judgmental. Most of us will run from silence. Through four or five decades of living and loving and working and arguing and making our way in the world, those of us entering or well into middle age have accumulated a lot of inner noise, and it speaks to us constantly—voices we don't know how to silence, memories of failures, daydreams of successes that never were, the near-continual recriminations that remind us we haven't lived up to other people's expectations, much less our own. I doubted it could be any different for this man.

"I see," I said. "You have a lot of silence, eh?"

———

As I sit on a bench in the curve on Spring Hollow, I wonder if it's starting to rain, but realize what I hear is debris falling from the trees, plopping around me. More dots on the canvas of silence. And I hear the silence, too.

I think about Julian of Norwich. We know so little of her life, which straddled the fourteenth and fifteenth centuries. We know she had her "showings," her revelations, in 1373, and we know she eventually became an anchoress at the church of St. Julian in Norwich, England, moving into a little apartment attached to the church. We know later she had further insights into those revelations, and she wrote them down for the sake of others. We know she was still there in 1413. That's about it.

But there existed a popular rule for anchoresses of that time, an outline for how to spend their hours and days, how to aim their lives toward God. There's good reason to think Julian would have followed this rule. She would have prayed seven times a day, like monks and nuns. She would have recited the psalms. She would have spoken breath prayers in silence, like the Jesus Prayer. She would have made vestments for the priests or paraments for her church. "That life is to be lapped about by silence," as one scholar describes the life of an anchoress. She would have had a window to talk with visitors, offer spiritual counsel, or let a servant know of her needs, but the rule devoted whole days to silence: every Friday, more frequent days of silence in Advent and Lent, all of Holy Week, and every day from night prayer to morning prayer.

A life lapped about by silence.

The second half of Julian's life was lived on the broad canvas of silence, and out of that silence the color of God's revelations of love began to show forth. The impact of her life and her teaching on God's love and care for creation are splashes of paint on the canvas of silence.

Remarkably, this reality of her life lived in silence mirrors one of the most beautiful aspects of her theology. For Julian, humans have forgotten who we are, where we come from. God is in, around, and through us; we dwell in God and God dwells in us so intimately that Julian could almost see no distinction. But we don't live out of the truth that God is the ground of our lives, the ground of our prayers, that who we are—our very existence—arises out of God, comes from God, and heads toward God, our beginning and our end. God is the canvas from which the colors of our own lives arise, on which the meaning of our lives takes shape. "It shows deep understanding to see and know inwardly that God, who is our maker, dwells in our soul; and deeper understanding to see and know that our soul, which is made, dwells in God's being; through this essential being—God—we are what we are." So thought Julian.

As I leave, I hear a toddler scream in the pavilion, about a hundred yards away. The scream feels close. It arises from the stillness, the silence, and is funneled toward me by the amphitheater of trees. And I think of Julian again, how her hearing from God, and offering to the world the consolation of her revelations, how that arose out of a life lapped about by silence—the silence of the ground of all that is: God. And how I, too, am rooted in the spacious silence of God's being, and whatever colors that appear in the second half of my life will emerge from a canvas that has a name and has a meaning: Love.

And I also believe this: that when doubts arise—whether doubts about the Vacation Bible School certainties I internalized as a child, or doubts about whether there really is divine ground out of which all arises, in which all is rooted—even those doubts can be brush strokes, appropriate parts of the picture, distinct aspects essential to the work of art that is my life right now. Even that belongs.

WALK 21

Another Kind of Silence

There is another kind of silence—not the replenishing silences, the "recreating silences," as Quaker mystic Thomas Kelly called them, but the silence of a soul that has lost its certainty, a soul that, as Julian says, has God as its substance, its ground, but feels like the ground is shaking as in an earthquake. I picture Peter, stepping out of the boat and finding the surface tension of the water sufficient to hold his weight—until it isn't, and the waves begin to swallow him.

There are times when I sense this situation is something to worry about.

Today, I'm learning: not necessarily.

This morning I had back-to-back appointments, which proved instructive.

First was a doctor's appointment to get my annual physical and the blood test required before I can have another year's worth of arthritis medication. I'd never been seen by Dr. Rivera, a thin woman, her collar bones framed by the open top of her rayon blouse, wisps of hair falling out of her bun and around her face. And laconic—she said only what was necessary and kept her questions short and sweet.

"I'm going to order tests to check your blood sugar and cholesterol, along with kidney function—because you *are* forty now."

Thanks for the reminder.

On the wall hung a body mass index chart, which I study every year while I'm here. When I spotted my weight on the horizontal axis and my height on the vertical axis, and followed the lines to see where they met, they rendezvoused in a band of yellow—the overweight range. Some quick math showed me I'd need to lose forty pounds to reach 175, the middle of the healthy range. I haven't weighed 175 pounds since I got my first driver's license. If I weighed that now, people would worry I'd contracted a wasting disease.

"You might want to think about losing ten or fifteen pounds. The weight can creep on as we enter middle age, and every pound makes a difference." We obviously weren't looking at the same chart. On the other hand, she didn't see a need for a prostate exam or a colonoscopy yet. "After all, you're only forty."

I left with referrals to a rheumatologist, since I might want to be under their care as I age, rather than a general practitioner; a urologist, to discuss my frequent need to urinate, a condition I knew to be characteristic of men of a certain age, but I thought that age was closer to sixty; and a dermatologist, to check the flaky brown spots on the dome of my belly.

As we discussed my weight, my pee schedule, my aches, and my skin, I remembered my father cursing the inconveniences of aging: the accumulation of medicines, the hearing aids, the pains that slowed him down, the waking to pee four times each night (and another thing he never mentioned: I remember coming home from college once to find brochures from the Mayo Clinic on erectile dysfunction strewn about an end table). But Dad was fifty-six when I was born. He had almost finished middle age by the time I knew who he was. Most of these bodily inconveniences started after he was seventy. How is it that I'm suffering them now?

"After all, you're only forty," she said. And that's the word I walked out deciding to remember, that so-sweet sounding *only*.

I drove straight from the doctor's office to Sister Anna's for spiritual direction. She answered the door and I went to the restroom, as I always do, knowing I have to sit for an hour; I don't want to dash to the loo mid-sentence. I inspected the Picasso print over the toilet—two hands clasping a bouquet of orange, yellow, red, and blue flowers—loving how these sisters chose a simple Picasso over something more obviously religious.

The subject of our conversation was my own growing reticence about faith, the laconic nature I seem to be acquiring. I talked for an hour (the irony!) about how increasingly, in intimate spaces—between two people, with my family—it's hard to talk about faith. The words evade me. I avoid praying at dinner; I ask Ginger or one of the kids to do it. When it's my turn to pray at faculty meeting, I find a prayer from a book or online. I can still write a prayer, if I have enough time, but the words don't flow like they used to, as if a damp blanket of silence has been tossed over the embers of my faith.

"If one of the kids walked in and said, 'Dad, tell me what difference Jesus makes in your life,' I'm not sure what I'd say, how I'd begin," I told her. And Sister Anna *smiled*. I seem incapable of making her believe any of this is a crisis. I can't conjure in her any bit of worry for my soul, at least not any I can detect. She accepted my disclosures with disconcerting, but also instructive, equanimity.

I realized I was replaying the conversation from months ago that ended in her suggesting I might be on the threshold of discovery, and I wondered how many times we'd had this conversation since. And still, she had not told me I'm not getting anywhere, so I might as well stop coming (as my piano teacher in high school told me after weeks of my not practicing), and she had not recommended a self-help book, or a psychologist, or a regimen of spiritual calisthenics, or a more experienced director who could solve my problem. And here's why: she doesn't think I have a problem.

The moon pulls the tide out each day, and the sand sprawls naked, bare. The moon calls the tide back in, and the sand shifts, reshapes itself beneath the water's turbulent to-and-fro. This is how it is; this is not a problem. And so with the soul, her smile and patience and equanimity seemed to say. Faith comes in, it goes out; it swells, it empties; it soars, it sinks. It's good to notice, and follow, and perhaps seek to understand, but there's no need to panic, and no prescription for a solution. Here's another mystery not meant to be solved.

What a contrast with my visit to the physician. Weight must be decreased, blood pressure monitored, arthritis pain eased, blood sugar lowered (I'll learn tomorrow it was a little high. "Try to avoid carbs and sweets," the nurse will say). All my stats must conform to the approved graphs and charts so that I can be pronounced a healthy middle-aged man. But it doesn't work that way with the life of faith. What seems like declension might be a natural transition, even the work of God. Our focus on solving problems in every other area of our lives must here, in the face of mystery, yield to trust.

And as we enter middle age, there's no reason to think the words and phrases and clichés that comprised our faith up to this point—like the ones my kids are learning at Vacation Bible School—should be the same ones a faith that will carry us through the middle decades of life will be built on. Their falling away, their rolling out like the tide, can leave a space of silence, a vacuum that may be uncomfortable to experience, but is nothing to be feared.

Which is a truth that Sister Anna, who has seen many individuals passing through these years, knows and can communicate with a gentle smile and a nod of the head. And who, when the hour is over, knowing we'll have another hour in a few weeks, and that nothing needs to be fixed between now and then, can pull out her calendar to set the date for our next chat.

———

Silas joins me on my walk tonight, skipping Vacation Bible School. His complaints seem legitimate—it's cheesy, too childish, the music is bad, and he already knows the stories and the simple lessons they are trying to teach. He seems to grasp what I am learning: how we express our faith to others and to ourselves shifts as we age.

I wonder if this walk could be an opportunity to engage him in a conversation about faith, to talk to him about the mystery of God—the mystery of God in my life. But the words are playing hide-and-seek. Instead, we talk about cedar waxwings, and what's making the trees creak and whine spookily in the oak forest, and the scarlet tanager that he proudly spots and points out to me, his lanky finger gesturing toward the bird, which we stare at together for several minutes in companionable silence. (Later I will learn that it wasn't mutually companionable. He was happy, he'll report to his mother, to spot the tanager, until I wanted to look at it for so long. Then he wished he hadn't.)

I discover that I'm okay with this situation. I will have to trust that the famous aphorism attributed to St. Francis—"Preach the Gospel at all times, using words if necessary"—is apt, and that I'm preaching some aspect of the Gospel as I walk in silence with my son. Or when he wakes early and catches me sitting in silence with the Bible flopped open in my lap. Or when we share a hymnal in worship and he hears my baritone voice crack when we sing *O, Love, that will not let me go; I rest my weary soul in thee*, and he watches a tear tumble down my cheek. This is my testimony, and I have to hope that he and his siblings, and maybe others, are able to hear it.

My heart is not hidden from him, I realize, even when my faith feels shrouded in silence. May I be like the heavens and the earth of Psalm 19, who declare the glory of God, even though

> *There is no speech, nor are there words;*
> *their voice is not heard;*
> *yet their voice goes out through all the earth,*
> *and their words to the end of the world.*

I don't need my speechless-voice to be heard that far. But maybe as far as the growing, inquisitive, curious soul, plodding along beside me?

Silas has my staff. Sometimes he uses it for support, but more often as a jousting lance or a light saber, which means I'm not completely silent as we walk up the hilly Oak Forest trail—my huffing and puffing join the chorus of the cicadas. But it doesn't feel a struggle. After all, I'm only forty.

WALK 22

Going Home, Finding Voice

A bench sits at first intersection of the Spring Hollow and Meadowview trails. Several feet to the right of the bench stretches a newly paved road, leading to an enviable outpost of private property nestled amid the nature reserve. If you're sitting on the bench, hikers coming up Meadowview from your left can startle you as they appear suddenly at the top of a steep incline.

I'm sitting on the bench in the evening. The sun pokes fingers of light between the branches. My walking stick leans against the bench, then rolls toward me and rests against my thigh. I'm taking time to remember the past few days. It was Ignatius of Loyola who refined and popularized a spiritual practice called the examen, a practice that encourages you to reflect on a particular period of time, give thanks for God's grace and presence over that time, and seek forgiveness for the ways you've resisted the call of love. James Martin, SJ, who might have been the world's most famous living Jesuit until Francis became Pope, offers a word that summarizes the heart of the practice: savor.

> In the examen we don't recall an important experience simply to add it to a list of things that we've seen or done; rather, we savor it as if it were a satisfying meal. We pause to enjoy what has happened. It's a deepening of our gratitude to God, revealing the hidden joys of our days.

And I'm savoring the memory of a recent trip home to Indiana to visit my mother, savoring the way my resistance was transformed into willingness, savoring the way silence helped me find my voice.

I didn't want to go. The reasons were so many and complex I'm not sure even I know them, but in the days before my trip home I felt an aversion, and the voice in my head sounded like a toddler, trying to negotiate his way out of going. Part of the aversion was to the traveling itself. Inexplicably, at middle age, I've developed a fear of driving through the mountains. The prescription bottle of Xanax on my dresser is there so that I can be a minimally tolerable passenger as my wife drives the van through West Virginia on family trips south.

"What are you afraid of? That the brakes are going to fail and we're going to fly off the side of a mountain?" she asked once.

"Yep, pretty much."

But I've never taken one, opting instead to sit in the back of the van with a blanket over my head. That way the kids don't see me cry, and I don't have to witness our plummeting.

I'm not supposed to take them when I'm the one driving, and I was visiting my mother alone. It's just a small part of West Virginia I needed to drive through, the narrow panhandle jutting north between Pennsylvania and Ohio, and I'd done it before. Still, the fear began to grip me.

There's also this: being home is hard. Since Dad died and my mom's mother died, Mom has become increasingly depressed and anxious. As a pastor, I had no problem sitting with people who didn't like their lives, for whom the most basic routines of life had become unbearable—getting dressed in the morning, paying bills, venturing a two-mile round trip to the grocery store. But now that my mother was one of these people, I found in myself a black hole where empathy should have been, a hole that emitted no light, but only negative energy, only frustration.

And petulance, especially when I have to sit and watch reruns of *Everybody Loves Raymond*, all the episodes of which Mom has neatly filed away in her mind like the crossword puzzles she cuts from the newspaper and saves in a folder next to her chair, and *Family Feud*, which she continues to watch even though she finds it a little "raunchy" sometimes. The last time my whole family visited, we were watching *Family Feud*, until the host asked the round-opening question, "What are you more likely to see at a bachelor party than at a bachelorette party?"

"Okay, kids," I said, "time to play cards in the other room."

But it might also be my resistance to witnessing her decline, seeing the woman who managed so much throughout my life—including a good bit *of* my life—come to the place where she can't manage to decide whether to wear a sweater when we take her out for lunch. Then there's the resistance to my own inability to manage this situation. Yes—that, too.

The morning before I planned to leave, having as yet failed to find a way out, I was praying downstairs, meditating on the hymn of Christ's condescension in the second chapter of Philippians: "Let the same mind be in you that was in Christ Jesus, who, though he was in the form of God, did not regard equality with God as something to be exploited, but emptied himself." It seemed a cruel joke. Here I was, agonizing about how not to have to visit my mother and watch reruns of a squabbling-family comedy, and answer her for the hundredth time that we *don't* watch *Everybody Loves Raymond* at home, and the stars were aligned in just such a way that I was reading a poem about Christ's willingness to let go of the prerogatives of divinity—*divinity*, people—to walk among humans, as a human, suffering the undignified death of the Cross. All in order that he might be with us in love. *Really?*

I have the bad habit of asking myself, when I'm praying with Scripture, *How does this passage touch my life right now?* That morning I didn't have to. In that moment I felt the aversion dissipate the way on some mornings I can see, from the chair where I pray, the fog over the Allegheny River valley slowly rise, thin, and disappear.

I persist in this habit of prayer, of reading about Jesus in the Bible and talking to him and sitting in silence with him even though I don't always know who Jesus is, or how he's at work, or why he would bother with me. Through all my doubts, I've never doubted that the way he lived matches my deepest longing: to be so utterly free of self-concern that I might be fully available to others in love. Jesus is the perfect teacher of that way. He doesn't ask for heroic self-sacrifice, or to go out of your way to suffer, or to scorn all earthly pleasures—after all, he had a reputation for enjoying some raucous company. But he might ask you to condescend enough to bear the burden of another's anxiety and fear and loneliness by simply being with them, by being present. Even your mother's. Even if that means watching *Family Feud*.

Who knew the imitation of Christ was so easy—and so hard?

———

Mystic and philosopher Simone Weil wrote, "Those who are unhappy have no need for anything in this world but people capable of giving them their attention. The capacity to give one's attention to a sufferer is a very rare and difficult thing; it is almost a miracle; it *is* a miracle." Lest I begin to think I managed to give such attention to my mother that weekend, Weil continues, "Nearly all of those who think they have this capacity do not possess it." I have no illusions that I have this capacity, but miracles are God's work, not dependent upon our own human capacities.

The first evening in Indiana, after 376 miles on the road—twenty of those the not-exactly-harrowing miles in hilly West Virginia—Mom and I ate pizza, which I picked up from our favorite spot. I did my best to stay mostly silent, to speak when spoken to, so that Mom would feel free to talk. I listened to her litany of fears and anxieties, chief among them at that moment: how to dispose of the pizza box. When I felt the frustration rising (*How can something so small as throwing away the pizza box cause paralyzing anxiety?*), I breathed in deeply and out slowly and channeled my inner Buddhist, mindfully embracing the moment.

And after dinner, instead of sitting on the couch with a book in my lap, signaling I had no interest in television, I watched reruns of *Everybody Loves Raymond* and mostly kept my mouth shut, except for the occasional laugh; the show does have its moments.

Part of me warned another part of me, *Don't go thinking you're a saint, because you're spending time with your mother!* That part was right. This wasn't heroic self-sacrifice. But I *was* spending time at home with my mom, offering what little I could give her: my physical presence, a listening ear, my attention.

———

Were those moments of silence—that effort at companionship, the willingness to set my book aside and be with my mother—what allowed her the next night to mute the TV, reminisce about Dad, and grieve her own mother in my presence? Were they what allowed me to find my voice, to finally speak?

She told me how hard it was to sit each night, facing the empty blue chair that matches her own, where Dad used to sit. She told me how much she missed her mother, who died at ninety-eight, and who, in the last years of her life, moved into a senior living apartment just a couple miles from Mom; how they talked on the phone each night, called each other during Indiana Pacer basketball games, during Colts football games; how, when one of them saw the moon out of her window, she'd call the other and, from their separate spaces, they would look at the moon together.

She told me that the day before Grammy died, family gathered in her hospital room, and my uncle told her that in heaven there would be a mansion just for her and streets of gold and family waiting. As a Methodist, Grammy was never burdened with biblical literalism, so she asked (according to my mother), "Do you really believe that stuff?" though I have trouble imagining Grammy using the word "stuff." Mom told me all this staring into the middle of the room. And then she turned to me.

Raymond and his mother were pantomiming an argument on the muted TV, as if playing charades. On the table in front of me sat a stack of books, topped by Mom's green bonded-leather Bible, with a book mark, a list of hymns for her funeral, and a couple photos sticking out. I doubt she'd opened the Bible in years.

"Do *you* believe that stuff?" she said.

Sometimes in the winter the windshield wipers on my car freeze. When they do, I turn on the defroster and wait as the air heats the window and slowly melts the ice trapping the wiper blades. I can see the blades trying to move, hear the motor fighting against the ice until they spring free, flinging shards of ice over the car and onto the road.

That's what my spirit felt like in that moment. I didn't need to rummage through a book for an answer or ask to be excused so I could think about her question and compose a reply. She wasn't asking Roger the theologian, or Roger the pastor, but Roger the son: "What do *you* believe?" And that Roger had an answer.

"I don't believe there will be literal streets of gold and mansions—though I'm open to being surprised. And I don't know if we'll recognize one another. But I do believe that we will be alive, together, in God, and we will know that we, and others we love, are okay, complete, whole."

She looked at me thoughtfully for a moment, then fumbled with the remote and unmuted the TV.

———

If right now, as I get up from the bench, marveling at how much change and gratitude one weekend can hold, James Martin, SJ were to hike up the hill to my left, appearing out of nowhere, and tell me that what I noticed in this little examen was God's Spirit at work, massaging a situation, and that I had been able to bend with the Spirit and finally find my voice because in the silence I'd been not only available to Mom but to the Holy Spirit at the same time—well, I'd be surprised to see him, and I'd wish I had one of his books to get his autograph, and I might even ask him to sit a spell and let me pick his brain about Ignatian spirituality.

But I wouldn't say I thought he was wrong.

— TRAIL EIGHT —

Finding Freedom within a Frame, Part One

You have to "espouse" reality rather than unreality, the actual limits of where and who you are rather than the world of magic in which anything can happen if you want it to.

–Rowan Williams

The practice of stability is the means by which God's house becomes our home.

–Jonathan Wilson-Hartgrove

WALK 23

Live Welcoming to All

Thursday, August 25, 6:20 p.m. Seventy-five degrees and seventy-five percent humidity. Small cumulus clouds bustle past on a cool breeze.

Native Pittsburghers inch open their front doors in weather like this and recoil from what they would call a "blast" of humidity. But someone who lived in North Carolina for fifteen years and still vacations there at the beach each summer—he would know better. He would say he can already taste a hint of fall.

While weaving along Fairview Road's two miles of curves and hills, muttering away about the stupidity of people who choose to jog along this road, I hear a story on NPR about yesterday morning's 6.2 magnitude earthquake in Italy that killed over two hundred people. The report notes the psychological difficulty of such devastation, especially for the elderly. "Many have lost everything in the disaster," reporter Eleanor Beardsley says. I think about my visit to Indiana last week, and the difficulty my mother is having, though her losses are gradual.

I can't imagine having all of my belongings instantly ripped from me, even though for years I have longed for simplicity, for a severe reduction in the things I own. This desire cohabits uncomfortably with an acquisitiveness I am only now discovering, a tendency to imagine having more—a fancier car (more specifically, the blue Audi I see around the neighborhood), a larger house, a deck off of our dining room to better enjoy summer evenings like this one. The urge to acquire and the urge to simplify wrestle like Jacob and his night visitor. Which will win? Which will limp away?

I have not been blind, over these past several months, to the fact that creation itself does not know how to possess. The squirrels collect their acorns, the nuthatches cache their food in the crevices of bark, but we would be projecting to say they are greedy, that they accumulate for accumulation's sake. They have a native sense of enough. Show me an animal with a sense of entitlement, and I'll take off its mask and reveal the human underneath.

Creation does not grasp. The apostle Paul tells us to imitate Christ's humble releasing of the prerogatives of divinity, the releasing that led to the Cross. "Let the same mind be in you that was in Christ Jesus." Paul is counseling *imitatio Christi*, the imitation of Christ. But maybe Christ himself is performing an *imitatio creaturae*, an imitation of creation, of its unselfconscious being without owning or grasping, without trying to possess.

A band is practicing in the screened-in room where we pick up our produce on Tuesdays. A catering van is parked nearby, and a blue sign-in tent stands in the front yard. Small trees near the tent have dropped a circle of leaves, intimations of fall in these late August days. I've learned to expect the feel of fall around here in earnest in September. I guess the two cool nights this week were enough to whisper to these trees, "I'm coming."

Midlife is a full season, in many ways overgrown, sometimes with luscious life, sometimes with weeds—our children not yet fully grown and needing more and more of our attention; our parents beginning to see decline; work pressures mounting even as boredom with the same-old-thing blooms—so full it might be useful to pause and ask: What are the hints, the signs in midlife, that letting go needs to happen? Not hoping for a Job-flood-earthquake-cancer-diagnosis-like ripping away, but for hints, calling us, like the cool breeze, to a deeper freedom in the midst of life's fullness.

The thirteenth-century Christian mystic Mechthild of Magdeburg wrote, "How should one live? Live life welcoming to all"—a lesson I long to learn. It's hard enough for me to live welcoming to myself and to those closest to me. Frustration and impatience born of proximity seem easier to welcome. Perhaps it's not my possessions this pre-fall breeze is inviting me to release, but the resentment, impatience, and frustration that make me chafe against the fullness of midlife, rather than welcome it.

The bridge over Harts Run is strewn with brown oak leaves and curled maple leaves, their silver sides upturned like cold waving hands. Some teeter on the edge of the bridge, not yet ready to give way completely and float down the run's gentle rapids.

I walk on, quicken my pace, climb out of the valley, and turn off of Spring Hollow onto Meadowview. The path narrows, weeds crowding in. It looks spooky, like Yoda's swamp-dwelling. The poison ivy is loving climate change: more warm days, more humidity.

I don't know why I'm walking so fast as I reach the farthest point from the nature center, and double back, climbing quickly through the pine stand. I step over a tree growing with what looks like scales and moss and fungi. My heart races, skips beats as I hurry. By the time I reach the bench, the sweat is rivering down my cheeks and neck, burning where I shaved with a dull razor this morning. The sweat reminds me that fall is not yet here.

But just now: the breeze again, so generous this evening, it evaporates the sweat from my face and cools my cheeks. This I welcome. And I can almost hear it whisper what it has whispered to the leaves in front of the nature center and the silver-maple leaves on the bridge, "I am coming, the season of freedom, the season of letting go."

Which is a necessary prelude to the season of receiving, of welcoming all.

The party is in full swing. The band—a fiddle, banjo, guitar, and a couple of singers—is covering Alison Krauss's "Restless." The crowd mills as the gloved caterers sit on the edge of the open van, waiting for the signal to serve the meal. The sign on the van announces, "Since 1979"—since I was four.

A man walking from the parking lot to the sign-in booth is dressed for a cool summer evening, as if the breeze has whispered to him, as well. He's wearing salmon shorts, a blue oxford with sleeves rolled up, and leather loafers without socks, boasting his lack of tan lines. A line is forming at the booth where a woman in a leg brace offers nametags. Three large prints displayed on easels signal that this is a fundraising event. I can see a new parking lot on one, new or renovated buildings on the other two—I can't tell from where I am—but I can see computer-generated images of children running around the structures.

Voices and laughter and loud music seep through the screen walls, and I imagine another party: the feast of Belshazzar, the Babylonian king in the book of Daniel, who sees strange writing on the wall. Daniel interprets the message for him: God has weighed him in the balance and found him wanting; that very night his life would be required of him.

Few of us receive so clear a warning of such a sudden letting go. Ask the hundreds still buried in the rubble in Italy.

Ask the nun, who was just found alive after being trapped under debris since yesterday morning, the nun who texted "Adieu, forever" to her friends and family, the nun who now gets to welcome living another day.

WALK 24

It's Close

O kay Pittsburghers, I owe you an apology. It *is* humid.

This morning, when I opened the front door to take out the dog, a blast of hot, humid air hit me in the face, like a burglar lurking outside the door, waiting to muscle his way into the house. If not for the lack of a briny bouquet, I might have thought I was back on the North Carolina coast. Any intimations of fall have scattered. Summer's back, at least for now.

As I stood impatiently in the yard, commanding the dog to "hurry up"—our family's euphemism for the dog's doing his business—I remembered what my mom used to say to describe this feeling of stifling, humid air. She'd say, "It's close." The expression puzzled me. *What's close?* But the Oxford English Dictionary has cleared things up. This use of "close" to describe weather comes from the Latin *clausum*, which means "closed, shut," past participle of the verb *claudere*, "to close or confine." Close air feels "like that of a closed up room; confined, stifling, without free circulation." The first uses of this word to describe weather appear in the sixteenth century in conjunction with other adjectives, like "sultry" and "hot."

Not often around here do we get to say it's sultry, but today? Yes. No breeze; hot, sticky air; it's *close*.

Now I wonder: might that word also name what midlife feels like for many—like being in a closed-up room, confined, without free circulation?

The heat doesn't stop us, at least not three of us. Ginger and Simeon have already gone to the pool, which has hired a DJ for tonight and extended its hours. Silas, Mary Clare, and I will join them for a late evening swim after our walk, during which I will be assaulted by the deafening refrains of songs I've never heard. And I will feel old.

We head up Spring Hollow toward the twin oaks marking the entrance to the path that winds into the valley. I call ahead to Mary Clare, advising her to watch out for the trolls that guard the path between the trees, but she presses on, heedless of my warning. The only things slowing her down are the gnats, which she slaps on her shoulders and rubs off her arms.

But Silas reprimands me. "You should be quieter," he says. "This is a nice place because it's a *quiet* place."

We turn onto Violet, a short-cut to the pond, and as we walk we see juvenile American toads, warty web-footed little monsters, like hopping dots decorating the path. These toads converge on the pond in April to breed, and then, having multiplied, fan out through the woods in the summer. The image of them crawling out of the pond to overrun the nature reserve could inspire a horror movie—if they weren't so cute.

Mary Clare begs me to grab one so she can hold it, and I remember something writer Lisa Purpura once claimed about the appeal of miniature things: they call for our attention. "Sometimes," she writes, "we need binoculars, microscopes, View-Masters, stereopticons to assist our looking, but mediated or not, miniatures suggest there is more there than meets the eye easily." But Mary Clare doesn't need any of those tools to investigate these miniature lifeforms. She only needs a dad with quick hands who's willing to bend over.

I try several times to capture a toad, but each time it jumps through the prison bars of my fingers, until I finally cup my palm, trap the toad against the ground, and close my fist around it. Mary Clare holds her own cupped hands out to me like a bowl, and we manage a successful transfer. Now the orb of her small hands encloses the *anaxyrus americanus*, like a prize trapped inside a happy meal box.

We hurry to the nearest bench, and Mary Clare squeezes between me and Silas. "Are you ready to look at it?" she asks.

The expression "it's close" reminds me of Edgar Allen Poe's short story "The Cask of Amontillado," which calls to mind another word related to *clausum*: claustrophobia. In that story the ironically named Fortunato is chained in a small vault, then sealed in block by block by the vindictive Montreso, until there's no opening, no way out. It's a story in which Poe mines his own fear of being buried alive to produce psychological terror.

I wonder if midlife is the time we are most likely to feel closed in, cut off, confined; the time we are most likely to develop claustrophobia, not a literal fear of small places, but an anxious reaction to the sense that the very building blocks of our lives—spouses, jobs, children, home ownership, sports team loyalties, all those things which once we strove to acquire and promised our undying dedication—have themselves become prison walls.

Granted, the Poe allusion rings melodramatic, but research in the growing field of the psychology of happiness and well-being is suggesting the answer is yes. Even if the trope of the midlife crisis is overblown, studies suggest that a person's sense of well-being, life satisfaction, and emotional health reach their lowest point in their mid-forties.

I remember an article in *The Atlantic*, in which Jonathan Rauch surveyed the available scientific data to discover the real roots of the so-called midlife crisis. He found evidence of something called the happiness U-curve, the nadir of which occurs, on average, at age forty-six. Researchers detected the curve even when they factored out other variables like family situation and income, suggesting the phenomenon might be correlated with age and not with the stresses and strains of midlife, though life circumstances can ameliorate or exacerbate the curve's effects.

Rauch interviewed a number of friends and acquaintances, asking them to put words to their experience of the nadir. As I read, I noticed the language of confinement. One forty-seven year-old friend of Rauch's, having just received tenure in an academic job, was surprised at how bad he felt. "Instead of feeling satisfied, he felt trapped. He fantasized about escape," Rauch wrote. Rauch himself, objectively successful in his forties, felt he "needed some nameless kind of change or escape." Rauch also quoted Gail Sheehy's book, *Passages: Predictable Crises of Adult Life*—the book that perhaps did the most to make the notion of a midlife crisis part of our cultural currency—describing the stereotypical everyman at midlife: "He blames his job or his wife or his physical surroundings for imprisoning him in this rut. Fantasies of breaking out begin to dominate his thoughts." Again: confinement and escape.

But this feeling doesn't constitute a crisis in itself. Rauch wanted to free the phenomenon of the midlife nadir from negative judgment by showing that it is a natural part of aging, not a blameworthy moral failure. If a crisis comes, it comes when we impulsively attempt escape: we walk out on a good marriage, pursue a chemical release, quit a career, or drain a bank account (when I have my midlife crisis, I'm going to buy a blue Audi). To make matters worse, people in midlife tend to underestimate the potential that things might get better, according to Rauch. The light at the end of the tunnel shines too dimly. "[M]iddle-aged people tend to feel both disappointed and pessimistic, a recipe for misery."

In other words, claustrophobia sets in, and energy turns to clawing fruitlessly, sometimes destructively, against the confining walls.

Silas and I lean in, and Mary Clare glances at each of us to build suspense. Then she slowly parts her thumbs until we can see the toad. Stuck on its back, it's displaying its milky belly. But when Mary Clare opens her palms a little wider to get a better look, it has the room it needs to right itself and spring free. It flies from her hands and onto the path. We watch it hop away.

I wish Rauch could have interviewed my Dad about his fifth decade; I wish I had. Would Dad have used words like trapped, confined, or escape to describe what led to his own leaping free?

He was claustrophobic, literally. He claimed it came from spending time in the Army Air Corp during World War II as a bombardier instructor, trapped in a plane for hours a day above a California desert, and it worsened as he aged. He wouldn't wear crewneck sweaters or undershirts; he detested any stifling clothing. A ministroke in his seventies meant he needed the occasional MRI, but he couldn't tolerate even an open-sided one. They canceled one MRI when he refused to enter the machine, and he wouldn't schedule another until he was promised sedation. When he and Mom returned home after that MRI, Dad was still woozy, and Mom couldn't get him into the house, so she asked the man who lived across the street for help. The next day the man's young son was visiting with my mom on the front porch and told Mom excitedly, "Guess what! Yesterday my dad had to help some woman get an old, drunk man out of a car!"

Claustrophobic—is that how Dad felt when he divorced his first wife in his early fifties and married my mom, fourteen years younger than he? I know so little about his first life, his first family, my three half-sisters. I do remember him saying that he was drinking too much, partying too much, that he was sliding toward alcohol dependency. Part of his leap must have been to escape that. But was there more?

My Dad was already past midlife when I knew him. From all outward appearances, he was settled, content with the routines of his second life: ushering in church on Sundays, mourning successive Cubs' losses, playing golf with his family—he never played with anyone else. About once a month he'd drive us to the Hong Kong Inn in Indianapolis, where we'd order the dinner for two, make a couple additions and a substitution, and I'd order a grilled cheese. He came home from the office every day for lunch, and again at 5:30 in the evening. He read the paper, ate dinner, watched the news, and then did it all again the next day, seemingly satisfied.

I regret there's so much about the inner life of that man that I don't know. And I think I wish I could ask, though I'm not sure, "What were your forties like? Was the leap inevitable? Was it worth it?"

One thing these walks have allowed me to see clearly: I don't want to dart. I get restless, yes. I check the job pages too often—is twice a day too often?—and complain that, dammit, I've got to wash the dishes again, but there doesn't seem to be a door about to close, about to seal me in a pressurized cabin called my life. Still, I have my dad's claustrophobia. I had my first attack on an airplane. Could there be a gene for this too? Can patterns be passed down? It's hard for me to imagine that

I could ever look at my life and decide to dash, to start over, to seek a *tabula rasa*. No, I don't think so. But did Dad think so at forty? The nadir, if the research is right, is still a few years away.

Maybe I should start saving for that Audi now.

We reach the pond, and I hear a familiar rattling. I look up to see a belted kingfisher circling above. It doesn't approach the water, never hovers over a spot before plunging in to claim a goldfish. It just circles, like Yeats's falcon, turning, turning. This is what freedom looks like. There, in the open sky, above the trees, tracing a widening circle against a blue backdrop, the bird seems the opposite of *clausum*. Appearances, though, are deceiving, both the appearance of confinement and the appearance of freedom. Often, what looks like freedom is a prison, and sometimes confinement is truly liberating.

At least that's what's suggested by another word related to that family of "closed, shut" words: cloister. I can't forget that Christianity's minority report—especially in a culture that bows at the altar of "life, liberty, and the pursuit of happiness," and imagines that anything like an obligation should be jettisoned—is that some people seek enclosure as the way to true liberty. The monastic Christian traditions tell us that the walls of the monastery and the convent, the stability of routine, the bumping into the same people every day—these "confinements" outline the space in which God's Spirit can liberate the soul to move toward its truest, highest end: the love of God and the love of others in God.

This is what Thomas Merton learned—the heart of the monastic vision—and he wrote more than fifty books to help those of us outside of the monastery learn it as well. Only in the monastery with his brothers and in the hermitage alone with God could he be free, could he become who he was meant to be, could his heart of love and his message of freedom in union with God reach beyond the walls of the cloister, reach around the world.

Reach *me*.

I don't have bells ringing seven times a day. I don't have someone reading from the saints and the Scriptures during meals, don't have routines of manual labor (except those dishes), don't have hours of meditative silence, but I do believe I can approach my next years and slide toward the nadir with a new perspective, one that helps me see that the people who are here with me and the obligations that I have allowed to bind me and the ones that will someday bind me, might be not a confining prison, but might circumscribe the space and create the conditions in which I might discover what I long for: the freedom to love, the freedom to become who I'm meant to be.

Another way of putting it: freedom needs a frame.

WALK 25

The Way of Blessing

This morning the kids stood ready at the door, even Mary Clare, who didn't have to leave for another hour. They carried colorful backpacks and sported fresh haircuts. The boys clutched lunchbox-coolers, which I'd dutifully filled with sandwiches, clementines, cheese crackers, and miniature cucumbers—their lunch fare for the next nine months. Before we went outside for Ginger to snap the annual first-day-of-school pictures, I stopped them. Not to ask them if they were forgetting anything. Not to move a stray hair or wipe a milky grin. But to bless them.

Last night I remembered a blessing I'd written two years ago for the start of school. I'd just returned from a weeklong retreat on Celtic spirituality, and I was eager to practice the Celtic way of blessing, to invite the ever-present Triune God to make the divine presence palpable in the particulars of the day, to open myself to the sacramental dimension of reality. So I searched through old journals until I found it.

They stood there, maybe remembering this from two years earlier, maybe not, or just humoring their silly-old-goat-of-a-dad, hoping he'd get on with it. They didn't flinch, or whine, or act embarrassed as I held my journal in my left hand and raised my right hand over them, and Ginger put her arms around them like a mother hen covering her chicks with her wings, and I read:

> Gracious God, bless Simeon, Silas, and Mary Clare, as they head back to school. May they have the gift of friendship; the joy of discovery; the confidence that they are loved; the pleasure of gaining knowledge; the humility to know when they don't know; eagerness to show kindness to others; perseverance to finish difficult tasks; and a sense of worth that comes from knowing what matters most about them is not the grades they make, the friends they have, or the praise they receive, but that they are Yours and You love them. Amen.

I choked up at the end. I often struggle to say what I feel, my emotions float so close to the surface. That might be one of the reasons it's hard for me to talk about faith more explicitly, not because I don't believe, but because, sometimes—always a surprise to me—I believe so deeply, and I don't want them to think I'm the foolish dad who cries all the time. *There he goes again*, I imagine them saying.

Now, as I leave for my walk this evening, after a quick pizza dinner at the classic Pittsburgh restaurant Primanti's, where every Tuesday night a balloon artist twists balloons into creations for kids (we left with a bow-and-arrow and two swords), I believe I know why that blessing I wrote came back to me, why the urge to bless is resurfacing. The way of blessing might be the way that midlife-as-confinement can be transformed into the frame in which I'm freed.

Maybe the Celts have something to teach me about muddling through midlife's uprooting, for they specialized in how to live in a divinity-infused world, abandoned to the Spirit's encompassing presence. And they are teaching me, through their practice of *peregrinatio*, which means "journey." But not just any journey.

You could be forgiven for mistaking *peregrinatio* for a pilgrimage, a holy trek with a set destination, undertaken for a specific religious purpose. But those on a *peregrinatio* journey with no settled destination from the start, with no way to know in advance when they will have arrived. The Celtic journeyers sometimes set out in *coracles*, small rudderless boats, and went where the winds of the world and the waves of the sea and the unpredictable breath of God took them.

You could also be forgiven for fantasizing how, in midlife, this kind of journey would offer a tempting escape, provide the fresh, the new—the very thrill midlife often lacks. But that's not the point of *perigrinatio*, either.

As I'm learning, the true beauty of the *peregrinatio* rests not in physical wandering, even if this has some appeal. As Ester de Waal writes, "Ready to go wherever the Spirit might take them, seeing themselves as *hospites mundi*, 'guests of the world,' what they are seeking is the place of their resurrection, the resurrected self, the true self in Christ, which is for all of us our true home." And *that* journey—the journey to our truest homes, our lives hidden with Christ in God—can transpire whether we travel the globe or never leave the county of our birth.

The home that is the true self in Christ is no further than the mailbox, the school board meeting, the sick kid's bedroom in the middle of the night; no further than the congregation that meets up the road on Sunday mornings, the homeless shelter where you serve a meal. No further than the hallway on which you and your colleagues prep your classes and write your books. No further than the frame that is your life now, even a life in its middle.

Every day, when your feet hit the floor and slide into your slippers and you shuffle into the kitchen to pour the coffee, you are already in a coracle, this tradition teaches, on an adventure into the unknown, however known it seems. *Peregrinatio* in daily life invites a shift in perspective. We might be wired for novelty, but the old and familiar is as novel as the new. Each moment is a fresh, fathomless mystery, a wave we've never ridden, a sea we've yet to sail.

And all of this, just from the bed to the coffee pot.

I remember, from that retreat and from my reading, that one of the ways Celtic people experienced ordinary life as *perigrinatio* was through the practice of blessing. In the nineteenth century, Alexander Carmichael recorded and translated the prayers, songs, and blessings he heard among the Scots, blessings that had been passed down from generation to generation in an oral tradition that conveyed the spirit of ancient Celtic Christianity—blessings for journeys, tools, life passages, and daily activities. Each task one undertook, each tool one handled, each face one saw of friend or foe or stranger, became an opportunity to recognize Christ and partner with God in blessing the world, became a chance to share in divinity.

These not-so-ancient nineteenth-century Celts walked daily the same roads and performed repetitive tasks, but those quotidian routines became the coracles in which the journey to true self, encompassed by God, took place. The way of blessing made it so. A favorite blessing of mine is this one for the milking of a cow:

> Bless, O God, my little cow,
> Bless, O God, my desire;
> Bless Thou my partnership
> And the milking of my hands, O God.
> Bless, O God, each teat,
> Bless, O God, each drop,
> That goes into my pitcher, O God.

A routine has a freshness, an infinite depth, a sacramental quality, when seen through blessing—no longer a constricting routine, but a doorway into joy and freedom.

Can this path of blessing train my vision to see each day—and each decade—as the playground on which God's Spirit gaily tumbles, the dance floor on which the Spirit spins and leads, the page on which each moment God is writing a new sonnet of love and joy?

Carmichael's work uncovered a Celtic penchant for blessing tools, the prayers beginning with the phrase, "Bless to me, O God"—in other words, bless as I take and use. And so, as I remove the canvas bags from the back seat of the car, I find myself whispering, "Bless to me, O God, these bags that will carry the produce; bless to me the produce that will feed, strengthen, and delight my family—especially if there are peaches! And bless, O God, the workers at Dillner Farms, whose cooperation with you helped this produce spring from the earth, the workers who are fulfilling the commands of Genesis to till and keep the earth. But especially, thank you for peaches." The blessing just slips out of my mouth, not with the fluency of a real Celtic bard, whom God seems to have particularly gifted, but it comes from my heart.

After I load the produce in the car—including peaches!—I begin my walk.

"Bless to me, O God, this staff, on which I have leaned for eight months. Let it be a sign for me of the gift of your supporting presence. May I become one on whom others can lean."

The blessings don't stop.

"Bless, O God, these groundhogs—this one dashing across my path and into the thistle, and this one on the hill eating vegetation near its burrow. Bless their corpulence, their bushy tails, their wacky waddle, bless them for the smile they bring to my children's faces, for the wonder they inspire."

There's no time to craft these blessings as art; I'm just responding to the urge to see God in *this*, find God in *that*, thank God for *this*, join God in blessing creation.

"Bless the goldfish in the pond, glistening jewels suspended underwater. Bless the kingfisher who will eat them, and this mystery of the cycle of life: the gift your creatures are to one another in life and death. Bless, O God, the men and women who made this boardwalk on which I stand, that extends into the pond the way your grace and goodness extend into each life."

The last couple of times I've been here I have felt rushed, breathless trying to get through the walk, but not today. Today I amble without a plan. I won't cover as much ground, but I'm savoring the ground I do.

I see to my right, parallel to the path I'm walking, the Toddler Trail, which I've never walked. It begins with a few steps made of fence posts pressed into the ground. In my imagination I see preschoolers and toddlers, some still wobbly on their legs, waddling like the groundhogs, negotiating these steps with the help of a teacher. I bless them in my imagination, and the teachers who lead them and inspire their curiosity and grab their little arms before they trip on a root. I think of Jesus saying, "Let the little children come to me," of his blessing them, and I hope that the opportunity to walk this trail will become a chance for these kids to meet the One who indwells each leaf and bunny and groundhog and teacher, the One who created each leaf and bunny and groundhog and teacher, the One who, through each leaf and bunny and groundhog and teacher, invites them to love, calls them to joy.

By the pond, I sit on the bench beneath the bat box and notice a plaque for the first time: "In Memory of Joe Hannity." By sitting here, I become a link in the chain of blessing that didn't begin with Joe, I imagine, but with a parent or a grandparent who took Joe outside as a little one and aimed his head at the stars, gestured toward a jay, gathered acorns and leaves and rocks, and helped him arrange them on a shelf. Then he blessed his own children and grandchildren with trips to this place and walks around this pond, I imagine, so that they gave this bench as a blessing, which it is to me as I rest and reflect and reconnect with the way of blessing.

"Bless, O God, Joe, his family, those who learned from him the love of creation and this place; who provided rest for me upon the way, this break a small taste of my longed-for rest in you."

Without effort, the most famous passage from the breastplate prayer associated with St. Patrick comes to my mind, a fitting encapsulation of this way of blessing:

> Christ beside me, Christ before me;
> Christ behind me, Christ within me;
> Christ beneath me, Christ above me;
> Christ to the right of me, Christ to the left of me;
> Christ in my lying, my sitting, my rising;
> Christ in the heart of all who know me,
> Christ on the tongue of all who meet me,
> Christ in the eye of all who see me,
> Christ in the ear of all who hear me.

I know better than to think I can keep this prayer, this blessing, in my heart at all times, but I believe it can help me live in the cloister of my life with serenity. Because it's in my walking and sitting and rising and lying and eating and working that the presence of Christ, ever creating and recreating, also walks and sits and rises and works. And it's in the faces of those whom I meet, the same faces day in and day out—faces of my wife and children and colleagues and students and neighbors whom I encounter through the regularity of my routines—that I will see the Christ who makes all things new.

A yellow butterfly, freely floating, wobbling on the vectors of wind beyond its control, like a Celt in a coracle, comes toward me, and I think it's going to land on my staff. I hope it will. Instead, it flutters past and alights on a stalk of thistle not far away.

— TRAIL NINE —

Looking for God

Why wonder that you do not understand?
For if you understand, it is not God.

–Augustine

God Is the Ruler Yet?

I'm sitting on the "In Memory of Joe Hannity" bench beneath the bat house. Labor Day, nine a.m. Still cool in the shady places, though the bench sits squarely in the morning sun.

Geese—I hear them before I see them, honking their way across the blue screen of sky, seventeen of them tracing a lopsided "V."

On my way to the bench, along Goldenrod, I spotted a snail shell in the path, the kind Mary Clare adores and would beg me to gather and bring home to add to the pile of knick-knacks on her dresser. I turned it over with my staff to see if it was empty, and the snail, spooked by this intrusion, retreated into the shell—which seems a picture of one possible response to the intrusions and upheavals of midlife, especially those caused by the questions of faith you thought were settled: hide.

I believe I'm choosing a different path, one marked by engagement, a path of learning from the discomfort, or at least not fleeing it. And the discomfort has no better opportunity to teach than when the rudely interrupting questions are about God.

Yesterday in worship we sang a favorite hymn of mine, "This Is My Father's World," and I'm still carrying the tune with me, humming the melody and turning the words in my mind.

> This is my Father's world, the birds their carols raise;
> The morning light, the lily white, declare their Maker's praise.

This verse evokes the psalmist's claim that the "heavens are telling the glory of God, the earth proclaims God's handiwork," and I can imagine the poet of Psalm 19 and the poet of this hymn, sitting on a bench by a pond like this one on a late summer morning, penning their impressions of praise all around.

The half of the pond opposite me, near the pavilion, is still in the shade. It appears blanketed with a cotton sheet of mist. The mist glides effortlessly over the pond's glassy surface, perfectly still except for occasional ripples from fish bumping the surface. Insects glisten on the water like jewels embedded in glass. The rising sun inches above the trees, and the mist becomes like a vampire, retreating to the shade for survival. Some distance behind me a pileated woodpecker pierces the quiet with its obnoxious call, what the psalmist would hear as its unique declaration of praise.

Across the pond, near the pavilion: a toddler with his parents. "Bye, bye, worm," I hear him say, his voice conveyed through the air's pristine calm, and I instinctively miss the voice of my own children as toddlers, the natural way they, like this child, would speak to creation with unselfconscious abandon—familiarity even. These parents proudly repeat the phrase, as if it's the most profound thing they've heard, the key to understanding the universe. And maybe it is, maybe the boy can still hear the worm utter its praise as it inches along. "Their voice is not heard," says Psalm 19—except perhaps by toddlers.

Just then a helicopter motors past, likely on its way to St. Margaret's Hospital, the closest emergency room with a landing pad. Its voice drowns out all the sounds around me for a few seconds, but its sound is not praise. Thinking of the injured person on board, my mind skips to the next verse of that hymn:

This is my Father's world, O let me ne'er forget
That though the wrong seems oft so strong, God is the ruler yet.

God is the ruler yet: an image prominent in the Church's praise. It companions other images, phrases that form a little club, like "God is in control," like "God is in charge." They can mean many things, but it's hard not to picture a scepter-wielding God on a throne, barking orders; a dictator, always getting his way. They are the kinds of phrases evangelical leaders like Franklin Graham and Pat Robertson bandy about as they blame events like Hurricane Katrina and 9/11 on folks who don't bow to their moral vision. God is in charge, and this is God's wrath. What happens, they ask, when you take prayer out of schools, make abortion widely available, and bless same-sex relationships? Their answer: God reminds us who's in charge.

Tell that, I think, *to the man or woman or child in that helicopter, airlifted from the scene of a crash: Don't worry, God is in control. This is part of God's plan, maybe God's punishment.*

But when I sang this hymn, I wasn't in Franklin Graham's church; Pat Robertson wasn't the preacher. I was in my mainline Methodist congregation, where most folks would reject such pronouncements, and yet we still truck in slogans like, "God is the ruler yet." Sometimes we sing "Be Still My Soul," a song of trust, its message supported by the swelling melody of Sibelius's "Finlandia." That hymn promises that when the storms of life strike, we have nothing to fear, because the wind and waves still obey God, still obey the voice of the "one who ruled them while he dwelt below." *Trust, because God is in control.*

Now that seems to me like a first-half-of-life sentiment, matching our youthful sense of invulnerability, our perception, however inaccurate, that we, too, have control of our lives. After all, we are made in the image of God, right?

A dragonfly zig-zags an erratic path above the pond, its ancient form catching and scattering the sun's light in a million directions. The mist is now backed into the far corner of the pond, a last refuge before its inevitable annihilation.

Over these months of observing the ebb and flow of my own faith, especially those moments when I've felt my own hand losing its grip on God and thoughts of God's likely nonexistence have buzzed unpredictably, uncontrollably in and out of my mind, I have sometimes feared that my faith was mimicking this blanket of mist, that the clear light of reason and the winds of doubt would conspire to push back the shroud of misty faith, so insubstantial, that I wouldn't be able to hold on, until only a swatch would be left in the corner, like a memento. Or nothing.

What I've been discovering instead, through walking and writing and praying and paying attention, suggests the opposite: the doubt, the fear of losing faith—these are the mists being pushed back, not by the clear light of doctrine, not by blowing them back with the wind of a childhood faith, not by fanning them away with platitudes like "God is in control," but by the evanescent glow, the warmth of a Presence, whose nature and name is Love, as Methodist hymn writer Charles Wesley put it, a divine Love that found embodiment in Jesus, and continues to seek embodiment in us. A Love that holds onto us and gently invites us to reciprocate.

———

The sun is baking my blue jeans, so I stand and walk a few feet to the trail Violet. In the shade the temperature drops about ten degrees. The trail overlooks a valley and a creek, and I hear a wren gurgling in the valley, enjoying, I imagine, the cool water whose own gurgling the wren seems to imitate. When I reach the "T" where Violet meets Spring Hollow, I hear the toddler again, coming up the hill to my right, his father in the front, his mother carrying him. "We're getting higher," he observes, as they approach me. We exchange "good mornings," and they pass.

The child wears a straw fedora and clings with one arm to his mother's neck. Her right arm supports his weight, and I realize: a psalm just walked by—walked out of the pages of Scripture and showed itself to me, a living image of the prayer of the one who said to God in Psalm 63, "My soul clings to you, your right hand upholds me."

Love, reciprocated.

I cling, I grasp, sometimes not knowing what I'm grasping for in prayer and in life, but I still reach out, try to hold on. And sometimes I feel I have a solid grip on something, though that is increasingly rare. I often think of a poem by Denise Levertov, in which she recounts the experience of grasping for God, only to have her hand slip on the "rich silk" of God's garment. That slipping can occur anytime, of course—an image of a God can seem to vanish like a mist, or a God we thought was in control can fail to come through the way we'd expected, and we lose our grip.

But I suspect this losing-the-grip happens most in midlife, when so much else in life is changing. What I thought would be a linear progression of growth in faith is not that. Faith is supposed to get stronger through the years, right? The certainties more certain, the clinging more secure, the images of God that sustain in clearer focus. But it turns out we're not climbing a ladder of faith, straight up to the top, surefooted in every step we take.

My soul clings to you. But sometimes I lose my grip.

Levertov's poem continues, suggesting that, though she has lost her grip, somehow God still holds her. She can't feel it; she doesn't have warm experiences in prayer, no consolations. She feels nothing. And yet, by the last line, she can affirm, her darkness and aridity notwithstanding, that she is being upheld. The poem, I think as I'm standing at these crossroads, is a kind of riff off of Psalm 63, because in the end, she still believes, somehow: Your right hand upholds me.

This image of God calls to me. Not a God who is in control of all circumstances of my life, asking me to trust him more—because this God-in-control always looks like a "he"—trust he will make everything turn out right, but a God who, like the mother carrying her toddler, upholds my being with the right arm of love. Sometimes I feel it, sometimes I don't—that's the way of faith in these middle years, and perhaps until the end. But my trust is growing that, no matter how tight or loose my own grip is at any moment, any day, any stage along the journey, through any season of my life, God's grip on me remains secure.

As the family walks away, the toddler stares at me as long as he can. I, the observer, have become the observed. His stare is so intense—he won't break his line of vision until the path curves out of my sight—that I imagine him in a few moments pulling out his notebook, jotting a few words, and making a sketch of the strange creature with a staff, gray t-shirt, and blue jeans, so that when he gets home and checks his *Field Guide to Grownups*, he will be able to make a positive identification.

"Here Comes the Divine Image!"

I don't tell him the truth when he asks, don't confess to what I'm doing. No point in alarming people.

I'm sitting on a bench at one of my favorite spots: the intersection of Meadowview and Upper Fields. And I'm loving September. The sun is dropping behind the trees, the atmosphere is tinged with orange, a cool breeze blows, and I feel alert, alive, awake, like anything is possible—even noticing God.

I hear the man before I see him, huffing up Meadowview toward me, a man old enough that his midlife years trail behind him. He clutches a stick for support and is wearing leather sandals and a pale green t-shirt that says "Papa Gator" above an alligator applique stretched taut across his belly. When he reaches me, he pauses long enough to make me fear he might sit down for a chat.

"Birdwatching, eh?" he says, noticing my notebook and pen.

"Sometimes, but not today." With a nod, he moves on, crosses the road, and continues on Meadowview.

What if I'd told Papa Gator what I'm really up to? What if I'd said, "I'm hoping to spy the infinite depths of reality. I'm here to see God in all things. I'm trying to see God in *you*."

He might have quickened his pace to get clear of me or reversed direction, retreating to the relative safety of the main buildings. At the very least, my words would have guaranteed he'd leave me alone.

In January I started "doing the Spiritual Exercises," to use the lingo of the people who know about these things.

In the sixteenth century, Ignatius of Loyola wrote a guide for retreat directors called *The Spiritual Exercises*. Earlier in his life he had sought military glory and the attention of the ladies, but a cannon blast to the leg ended his military career. As he recuperated, he wanted to read the dime novels of the day, but he only had a life of Christ and a book about the saints. As he read and reread those books, he discovered an attraction to the lives he was reading about. He began wanting to follow Christ and to live like a saint. Imagining himself in the army of Christ, he felt joy and excitement; contemplating his old life of vain self-seeking, he felt distress. He took these movements in his spirit as a sign he was meant to follow Christ and spend his life "helping souls." One of the ways he helped others was by leading people through prayer exercises, based on his own experience of meditating on the life of Christ, to help them discern what kind of life God might be calling them to live, and to help them begin to "find God in all things."

Over the past almost five hundred years, thousands have prayed through Ignatius's exercises, hoping to discover an inner freedom, hoping to become capable of noticing and responding to God's presence in their lives.

And now I'm one of them.

—————

I'm near the end, the last meditation, and I've brought it with me today. It's taken almost nine months to get here. I've followed the life of Christ, prayed slowly through his Passion and Resurrection, and recorded my own inner responses to these meditations. I've engaged in what Ignatius called "colloquies," respectful chats with Jesus, Mary, and the saints. I've spoken to them and imagined what they might say to me in return. I've considered my gifts and vocation, asked God for the grace to grow in love, begged sometimes for inner freedom. I've wept in joy and grieved my slow progress. Now I'm at the end, where Ignatius's instructions tell me to ask for the grace to "love and serve the divine majesty in all things." I don't balk at this directive; it's all I really want.

Here are Ignatius's instructions:

> I will consider how God dwells in creatures; in the elements, giving them existence . . .

The setting sun, the breeze, the earth I feel crunching beneath my feet as I twist them about; the pebbles the kids always want to skip on the pond; the living water that trickles down Harts Run.

> . . . in plants, giving them life . . .

The trees behind me, all around me, the grass carpeting the paths and softening my footfalls; the tree that gave itself for this bench; the produce that grows at Dillner Farms and is brought here for my family's enjoyment and nourishment, even the kohlrabi and eggplant *(I must remember to pick up the produce).*

> . . . in the animals, giving them sensation . . .

The downy woodpecker, scratching his way to the end of a branch to find insects, the titmice warning their comrades of a snake or a hawk, the chickadee who hangs upside down to fetch some food from the underside of a leaf; the house finch caught in the briars in our front yard earlier today, which I held—so delicate, like holding air—that didn't struggle as I pulled briars from its wings and neck, until it felt free enough to wiggle out of my hand and hop away, not yet fully liberated.

> *. . . in human beings, giving them intelligence . . .*

The men and women who teach kids in the education center, the folks who volunteer in the gift shop, the people who clear the paths and lead the hikes; the farm workers who tend the produce and load it into boxes, even the ones who decided to grow kohlrabi, and the people who organize the distribution every Tuesday *(must remember to pick up produce!)*; Mary Clare, the way she slumped in her car seat last night on the way to urgent care, and the people who responded on Facebook to the picture I posted of her—"Praying," "Sending up prayers;" the staff at the urgent care facility who were so eager to close they said they couldn't help her and sent her to the ER at the children's hospital, where they would be able to give her intravenous fluids for her dehydration; the doctors at the ER who said they don't give IVs to little kids, *just get her to drink Gatorade*. And speaking of gators, Papa Gator, who had the wisdom not to tarry too long and talk.

> *. . . and finally, how in the way God dwells also in myself, giving me existence, life, sensitivity, and intelligence, and even further: making me his temple, since I am created as a likeness and image of the Divine majesty.*

This one takes me by surprise. I expected to be looking for God outside of me—but in me?

I look in wonder at my hands. They seem unfathomable, the loose skin sliding over the joints, the new wrinkles, so small, warts spreading on the knuckle of my right pointer finger, a scar on the tip of my other pointer finger, where I sliced it as a child trying to cut up an old pair of leather boots with sharp scissors, and then lied to my mom when she found a hundred bloody tissues in the trash because I was afraid of being in trouble—"I don't know how it happened," I wailed, as she held my finger under the faucet. These hands that have smacked the bottoms of my boys in anger and impatience, and cradled them for countless hours; these hands that have played the piano for years, hitting as many wrong notes as they have right ones, just as my life has.

And yet, God dwells in me? I am God's temple? *This*—these hands, this life—is what the likeness and image of Divine majesty looks like at loose in the world?

I began by asking for the grace to see God in all things. I didn't anticipate that "all" would include me.

Papa Gator has finished the Meadowview loop and reappears to my right.

"Still taking notes," he says. I can't tell if it's an observation or a question. I close my notebook and stand to continue my meditation as I walk. It's still light enough that his photochromic lenses haven't changed from their dark green. He is, if Ignatius is right about God being in all things, a sandaled theophany. A rabbi once said that every person has angels flanking them, clearing the way, announcing, "Here comes the divine image!"

Papa Gator: chaperoned by angels.

"I'm going to take your bench," he says.

I think, *The divine image is welcome to it.*

As I walk I hear screeching in the brush, see movement, branches shaking, leaves vibrating. *A bird I've never heard*, I think, until I see a three-striped chipmunk emerge from beneath the groundcover, its tail perpendicular, at attention. Then it returns to its foraging, using its God-given powers of sensation—a sign of God, Ignatius would say, along with its agility, its power of movement, its very life: divine life in motion. Maybe this chipmunk has angels, too, tiny little ones, chittering, "Make way, make way."

And I think I can almost sense them, almost believe they are here, alongside me too, despite myself, believe that God *is* giving me the grace to see what I didn't know I would be asking to see: the divine in me, the mystery at the heart of me.

One is so close I feel the hair on my arm stand up as it passes. I've never had an entourage, or never knew it, but here they are, announcing in a language I can somehow understand, "Here comes the divine image." They walk with me the rest of the way, politely declining to help carry the produce to the car.

— TRAIL TEN —

Finding Freedom within a Frame, Part Two

We want life to have meaning, we want fulfillment, healing and even ecstasy, but the human paradox is that we find these things by starting where we are, not where we wish we were.

–Kathleen Norris

WALK 28

Found Sabbath

I don't know how Joseph and Mary felt. How could I? I've never had my sleep interrupted by an angel telling me to pack my bags and hit the road in a hurry, to flee with my child for the sake of his life; never been warned to escape a dictator who wants my little one dead. But that's how the story goes in Matthew's gospel. An angel urged the holy family to escape—to Egypt, no less, in a recapitulation of Israel's history: God's family, God's son, had to flee *to* Egypt, as the Hebrew people did in Genesis, before a Pharaoh arose who knew not Joseph.

Obviously, not all escape is bad; some is even necessary.

I remember hearing a sermon that made this point. I wasn't in a sanctuary, unless you call the kitchen of the parsonage where we lived a sanctuary. It was early January, 2011, and I was washing dishes and listening online to a sermon recently preached at the Duke University Chapel by Rev. Sam Wells. Most people don't remember particular sermons—good preaching should be like the evening meal: you don't remember each sermon, but you hope that, cumulatively, they're nourishing. But I remember this one because it gave me permission to ask whether I needed to escape. "There's a lot in most of us that's longing for an escape. Some escapes are very good ones. The ability to relax can be important in creative kinds of renewal. Other escapes, like Joseph and Mary's, are vital ways of staying alive, staying sane."

I'm remembering that sermon today because I need an escape. Not the pack-your-bags-and-move-to-another-country kind; not the throw-up-your-hands and throw-in-the-towel kind we call a midlife crisis. I don't need an escape to save my life. I need one, even a brief one, from the daily debris that gets tossed into your soul and piles up, the little daily desolations that board the elevator of your mind until it's exceeded maximum capacity.

Four days ago, a police officer in Charlotte, North Carolina, shot and killed Keith Scott, the most recent in a string of police killings of African American men. Protests in response to the shooting have been chaotic and violent. Today the police announced their intention to release video footage of the shooting. I know, as a person of privilege, I could easily hide from this kind of injustice, and I don't want to do that. Still, a break from the news, a rest for my mind, perhaps?

In class this week I was teaching on the themes of true and false self in Christian spirituality. To illustrate the possibility of collective false selves, I played an NPR story about a white community hatefully fighting to prevent African American students in a nearby failing school district from being bused to their schools. In the wake of the Scott killing, hearing the story proved upsetting to some of my African American students. I felt horrible for not giving a warning, and guilty for not being more cognizant of how my students might react. Professor fail—another rider on the elevator who won't leave.

And this: a presidential election in less than two months, with a resurgent, emboldened, racist, and xenophobic right wing, hoping to embed their ideology in the White House by electing Donald Trump president. And Hillary's e-mails. There's that rider, too.

All aboard, going up.

I'm thinking of the jingle for Kit Kat: "Gimme a break, gimme a break, break me off a piece of that Kit Kat bar." But I need more than candy. And Egypt is too far away.

I am relying on two sources of authority to support my choice to allow my walk this evening to be the escape I need. Recent psychological research, reported in the *New York Times*, has suggested that a walk in nature "may soothe the mind and, in the process, change the workings of our brains in ways that improve our mental health." More specifically, time spent walking in nature calms the part of our brains that engages in "morbid rumination"—a phrase that feels oddly familiar. I've got research on my side. Take a hike!

I also have Jesus on my side. After a busy evening of feeding thousands, he escaped, took a hike, "went up the mountain by himself to pray." I knew there was a reason I liked this guy.

Even if he had to come back down the mountain, re-enter the fray, which he did because he hadn't been gone long before a squall began battering the boat the disciples were in. So he descended the mountain, walked to them on the water, and stilled the storm.

Escape. You don't have to escape your whole life. Sometimes you just need a few hours on the mountain alone.

Or on a bench on Vista trail, watching chipmunks.

The walk to the bench isn't doing the trick. Yellow and brown leaves speckle the paths, the colors of the nature reserve are a swirl of green and brown and blazing orange in the setting sun, and my mind tells me, *Be at peace; this is your favorite time of the year.* But my heart continues to race, and the morbid rumination persists.

I start to doubt the science and begin to wonder what Jesus was thinking about on that mountain. Maybe it wasn't a night of mystical bliss, but one of pacing, of worry. "Let not your hearts be troubled," he told his disciples once. But maybe his heart was.

When I reach the bench, I feel closed in, small trees and shoots and plants rising like a wall in front of me, like the closed doors of an elevator. Claustrophobia again—not the claustrophobia of midlife, but the claustrophobia of an anxious mind. As I sit, I feel my heart thumping in my chest, my blood throbbing in the tips of my fingers.

Then I hear two chipmunks behind me, squawking like angry birds. They run across the path, chasing one another into the brush. One comes back out eating something—a seed, a nut? The other reappears and gets chased off again. They are like comedians unwittingly rehearsing their routine before an audience—me. I hold perfectly still as I watch. To them, I might as well be part of the bench. And then I realize that as they had my complete attention, my mind settled; the elevator doors opened, and the riders disembarked. My rumination paused. The surprising, attention-grabbing fete of these chipmunks: to rescue me from my thinking, to help me just *be*.

Like grace, sneaking up on me. Like grace, cracking open the door of my dungeon. Like grace, making room for me to breathe, at least for a while.

And it happens again and again on the rest of the walk: the warbler I can't identify, the twenty-or-so other chipmunks I spot, the two ducks sliding across the surface of the pond, the groundhog who moseys through a maze of his own making to reach the water—all of them are part of grace's machinations to give me a little rest, which I gladly accept.

The word sabbath means "to cease." And that's what my mind has done, for the moment. Sometimes you find a sabbath; sometimes a sabbath finds you.

WALK 29

Running the Ruts

Silas suggests an evening at Squaw Valley Park. With tennis courts, two playgrounds, sand-pit volleyball, basketball courts, and a walking path, Squaw Valley delivers variety for a family of five with divergent interests. I, on the other hand, want us to walk together at Beechwood Farms, but I know making this happen will require fine-tuned negotiating skills.

We gather in the family room for the summit.

My opening gambit: "Let's walk for twenty-five minutes, and then you kids can play at the playground for another twenty-five minutes."

"But you can't throw a Frisbee there," Silas says, holding up the orange disc as Exhibit A.

True. I know Frisbee-throwing has to be part of the deal, though my shoulder aches just thinking about it.

"I'll throw it with you in the front yard for a few minutes when we get back."

With each offer, my walk time gets shorter, but victory, nearer. Ginger watches with arms folded across her chest and a silent smile on her face, showing her enjoyment of this bit of familial bartering. I can tell I'm not going to get any backup; I'm on my own.

Mary Clare is easier to win over. I just tell her I saw almost twenty chipmunks yesterday; she can't resist the allure of animal cuteness.

A few minutes later, the deal is done. We are traipsing up the hill in the front yard toward the van, happily unified in our decision to spend the evening at the nature reserve, and I'm congratulating myself on my diplomatic prowess. *The next president would be wise to appoint me Secretary of State—peace in the Middle East will finally be within reach.*

But in the van our unity quickly unravels. Mary Clare wants to play music from the old red phone she uses as an iPod, and chooses something Vacation-Bible-Schoolish. The boys revolt from the backseat, shouting in unison, "Turn it down!"

"No!" Mary Clare screams, determined to have things her way. She clutches the phone to her chest.

Simeon begs to listen to a popular acapella group, Pentatonix, which he has obsessed over for months, but Silas objects.

"I don't want to listen to Pentatonix. You always talk about how amazing they are." His tone drips with disdain. "And you play them all the time and I'm sick of them," he says, ending with a crescendo. Then he adds a coda. "And I feel the same way about *Hamilton*"—a nearly sacrilegious admission in our family. An argument in the back seat ensues.

"Stop hitting me in the head!" Simeon says.

"Silas, leave Simeon alone—don't touch your brother," I shout, glaring at them in the rearview mirror.

"I didn't hit him, I just did this," Silas says, bopping his brother in the cheek.

Ginger's smile has disappeared, and I begin mentally composing my letter of resignation from the president's cabinet. Peace in the Middle East will have to wait.

Yesterday I wanted to escape for an hour and find a little Sabbath rest in a world gone mad. Right now I want to rent an apartment on the other side of town.

When you find yourself mumbling under your breath about why you brought your kids with you, about what made you think this time would be different, about why you even had kids in the first place; when nine in the evening rolls around and you confront the nightly routine you've been following since what feels like the Mesozoic era—make sandwiches for kids' lunches, prepare the coffee to brew in the morning, brush your teeth, floss, take your medicine—and you want to hoist the coffee pot into the trash can; when you rub your palm over the fabric of your life, and what used to feel soft, inviting, and invigorating now scratches like burlap—that's a sure sign: you are normal, and susceptible, as everyone is, to the demon known as *acedia*.

The ancient Christian monks of the desert called acedia the "noonday demon." When a monk wakes in the morning there is energy, enthusiasm to face the day, but by midday the routines become tedious, hope dwindles, and he may wonder how he can possibly endure as the afternoon stretches out before him like a lifeless desert. The word acedia is often translated as listlessness or spiritual boredom, but really what names its power is the aversion to *now* at its heart. As the early Christian monk John Cassian said of acedia:

> This is a harsh, terrible demon, always attacking the monk, falling upon him at the sixth hour (mid-day), making him slack and full of fear, inspiring him with hatred for his monastery, his fellow monks, for work of any kind. . . . He suggests to the monk that he should go elsewhere and that, if he does not, all his effort and time will be wasted.

Under the influence of acedia, you begin to hate your life, your routines; loathing builds and you either want to give up or flee. Before you know it, you've run away from whatever you were doing—or were trying to find the energy to do—and have raced into the kitchen to rifle through the freezer is search of fudge-ripple ice cream.

The ancients called it the noonday demon because it struck at midday. But isn't midlife the noontime of our lives? So we shouldn't be surprised when acedia sneaks up on us here.

I know I'm suffering acedia when all my talk and good intentions and even belief about seeing God in the daily, finding the divine in the mundane, noticing God in the moment—when it all dissolves into the monochrome gray of routine. Even these walks—here I am on my twenty-ninth—are becoming routine, rote, something I have to do. They are lacking surprise. *Oh look, another bird. Yay.* I know exactly what Kathleen Norris means when she says, "The grip of acedia on the human spirit is such that even the great beauty of this land and seascape can be rendered impotent and invisible." When this beauty is masked, how can I possibly see the mystery at the heart of it all, or hear the Spirit speak through a squirrel or in the squabbling of siblings, as I believe the Spirit does? How can I feel God's presence when it all feels like *here we go again*?

And then I find myself trapped in a van or on a monotonous walk, and there's no ice cream anywhere close.

The grand vision to which I aspire—and which I have tasted, off-and-on—is expressed by Thomas Merton. I want nothing to be truer than what he once wrote: "It is God's love that warms me in the sun and God's love that sends the cold rain. It is God's love that feeds me in the bread I eat and God that feeds me also by hunger and fasting . . . . It is God's love that speaks to me in the birds and the streams."

> *And through the giggle of a six-year-old?*
> *The squeaking saxophone of a fifth-grader?*
> *The baked-goods of a sixth-grade son?*
> *The good-night kiss of a wife?*
> *The infuriating energy of a puppy?*
> *An aching arthritic shoulder after an hour of throwing a Frisbee?*

If yes, then I want to see this love and feel it and let it be seen through me. But acedia—boredom, frustration, aversion—can blind me to it and send me to Dairy Queen in a matter of seconds.

Cassian had not been in the desert for very long when acedia afflicted him. So, he went to Abba Moses, a wise, well-known monk, and told him that he wasn't able to free himself from acedia until he stopped what he was doing, left his cell, and went to visit Abba Paul. Abba Moses responded, "So far from freeing yourself from it, you have surrendered to it completely and become its slave. You must realize it will attack you all the more severely because you have deserted your post." Cassian fled the present, fled *now*.

He went to visit Abba Paul, no doubt, because fudge-ripple ice cream doesn't keep in the desert. I wonder if he considered buying Doritos.

Once the walk begins the bickering abates; freedom from the confines of the van has allowed the negative energy to dissipate. Mary Clare lunges into the brush and pulls out a stick about her height, its crooked, thick bark peeling off. She takes a few steps, using it as a staff, before she announces, "I'm up to the challenge," and then flings it back into the brush.

We follow the same relatively short route I walked yesterday. The kids and I sit on the bench from which I watched the two clowning chipmunks, but today none are willing to perform for an audience of five. Impatient, the kids run off, making enough noise to scare away any small animals that the quiet ones among us—Ginger and I—might otherwise have seen. This is the way it seems always to be when the five of us are here. The kids run ahead, fighting about who's going to be in the lead, as they have begun to do now, and Ginger and I linger behind.

But something alters our usual. Mary Clare starts to wheeze, her fall allergies and asthma conspiring to slow us down. Ginger listens to her breathing, an ear to her mouth and then her chest, and nods to indicate she detects a raspy wheeze on each exhale. We tell the boys to stop running so Mary Clare won't feel compelled to try to keep up, and—*mirabile dictu*—they comply. Within a minute the whole scene is transformed. Ginger and Mary Clare now linger behind, holding hands, and the boys are holding my hands—Simeon on my left, his soft, padded fingers interlacing mine, and Silas on the other side, holding on with his smaller, bony hand. The five of us walk slowly and quietly toward the playground.

To our right, a chipmunk bursts from the brush like a superhero leaping into the air, and lands two feet up the side of a tree. We observe it, and it observes us, before it jumps back undercover, and we hear it burrow away.

And I forget about an apartment on the other side of town. I want this to last forever.

I recently reviewed Barbara Bradley Hagerty's *Life Reimagined: The Science, Art, and Opportunity of Midlife*. She writes about the ruts we can fall into in midlife—relationship ruts, family ruts, work ruts, hobby ruts—and recommends changing things up. Enamored with brain imaging technology, she shares the scientific consensus: "The brain rewards novel activity and craves surprises"—which seems to me like a declaration that the demon of acedia is no demon at all, and we should heed the restlessness.

Hagerty writes, for example, about how marriages lose their romantic spark when they get into ruts—date night, *again*; movie night, *again*; watching Downton Abbey, *again*. She asks, "How can middle-aged couples keep their marriages fresh?" Her answer: novelty. "The brain rewards novel activity and craves surprises." To test her theory, Hagerty and her husband rented an RV for several weeks and motored across the country.

Her story has haunted me. Does it require a drastic—and expensive—adventure to inject renewed interest in a marriage, a job, a hobby, or a friendship? Does one need to escape the rut to appreciate it anew?

Then I remember those ancient monks. Their antidote to acedia costs less and requires no vacation leave. They put a premium on patience and perseverance, on just sticking it out, but they also prescribed manual labor to help make it through the desert of the afternoon. When the noonday demon strikes, and you want to flee your cell—go back to the city and take up your old trade or join another monastery—when the aversion to the present afflicts, whatever the present happens to be—whether praying the psalms or putting up with bickering kids—do something with your hands, they suggest, engage your body, right where you are, or pretty close by.

There's a saying from the desert about Anthony, the "Father of Monasticism," that illustrates this advice. In his struggle with acedia, he cried out to God for help. A little later, when he got up to wander about, Anthony saw a vision: a man sitting down to work—plaiting a rope—and then standing to pray, then sitting to work, then standing to pray. He knew he saw an angel sent by God to help him. "Do this and you will be saved," the angel said, words that filled Anthony with courage and peace. Without "deserting his post," as Cassian did, Anthony discovered he could stay within the rut, within the routine, but vary it slightly, engaging his body, using his hands, and thus persevere in prayer and work throughout the day.

That's what's happened on this walk, I realize. We didn't have to find another park, go bowling, or take a vacation to Yellowstone to gaze at the geysers, tired of each other and the same ole, same ole. A little variation, injected into the routine—Mary Clare's wheezing—slowed us down and caused us to recalibrate our present without escaping it. The change invited patient walking and touch—in this case holding hands—but it could have been running a hand across the bark of a tree, or walking barefoot in the grass. And we are once again engaged, delighted by the present moment rather than scheming to escape it.

I wonder if this principle might hold for other areas of midlife.

So you and your spouse watch a movie every Saturday night. Do you really need a cruise to reawaken the romance, rekindle the relationship? What if you start holding hands again during the movie, like you used to do, or take turns giving back or foot rubs? You could plait rope, I guess, but I'd try backrubs first.

Friday night has been family pizza night—with delivery from the favorite pizza joint—for how many years? Try making pizza together. Take turns stretching and rolling the dough, chopping the vegetables, placing the pepperoni on the pie instead of racing to a restaurant and dropping $100 on a meal, only to leave dissatisfied. Much of the time, the promise of reinvigorating a routine rests no further than our fingertips.

Here's the question I want to start asking when restlessness at the noon of my life tempts me: What little shifts, what "work," can I do here and now, *within* the routine structures of this life that grace has given me, to help me reinvigorate the routine, to see and love the present anew? After all, there's no money in the bank to rent an RV.

Merton says God is feeding me in this moment, anyway, so why would I send back the plate?

While the kids are playing, Ginger and I see two chipmunks scurry from the meadow, across the path, and up a hill near us. Like two kids, we skip over to investigate—I guess we can't resist the allure of animal cuteness, either. Already, here's something new. Usually I'm alone or with the kids out here, but here we are, the two of us, shoulder to shoulder, bending over like preschoolers on a fieldtrip, looking for chipmunks. What we see is a faint rut in the grass, the path the chipmunks follow each day to find food and water, their light-as-a-feather bodies bending the grass, leaving this groove.

Rut—it's such a pejorative word. "I'm in a rut," we say, the implication being that we need to get out of it. But the monks and this walk are showing me that there can be novelty within the ruts, and beauty, and space for growth in both patience and perseverance. There can be room to reimagine how we live in the rut. Not all ruts must be gotten out of, for God is in our ruts as well.

WALK 30

Being Mindful, Trying

Well, that's one way to interject some novelty into midlife ennui, I think. I hear on my way to this walk an interview with the author of a new book, a daughter's memoir about living with a father who was a compulsive liar, had a secret family, and robbed banks dressed as Mario from *Super Mario Brothers*. Sometimes, she says, she leaves that detail out when she tells the story because people start to laugh and stop taking her seriously.

That kind of double life would be hard to pull off. It's much more common to live a secret life through our fantasies and daydreams—the life of a CEO, rather than a manager; the life of one who has won the Powerball, inhabiting a fantasy world of wealth and fame; the life of a hermit—maybe not everyone's go-to secret life—or of a children's book author. So many lives our daydreams can lead us to.

On Goldenrod: it's 5:50 in the evening. A crisp fall breeze caresses my face. A thin cloud-cover, like a scrim, blocks the sun, diffuses its light. This is the first time I've worn one of my sweater-shirts this season, along with my black jacket.

I notice: the sound of crunching under my steps, the path strewn with leaves knocked from their strongholds by heavy rains over the two weekends since I've been here. My staff lands on one, decimating it. Lichen carpets four flat, gray stones that mark the beginning of the trail.

I feel: protruding roots under my feet pressing into my arches, and I imagine I am an enormous giant traipsing across mountain ranges.

I see: a squirrel in a walnut tree, eating a nut. I hear its nibbling, see its ears twitch, watch its paws spin the nut like a dowel on a lathe.

I notice: a couple sitting on the other side of the pond. I hear their voices and see him lean close to her. She wears a shawl, a southwestern black-and-white pattern, like the blanket I bought in Mexico twenty-five years ago.

I consider: walnut pods, like the ones we used to throw as children and smash against trees, that used to stain our fingernails, scattered here in the path like exploded ordnance, and I wonder how they got this way. Was it the force of the fall? Does an animal open them that way? Do children crush them beneath their feet?

Oh, those poor children, when they track the brown stain inside.

Then my mindfulness is stolen by intruding thoughts pulling me away, barging into the moment like a breaking news alert. The video was released two days ago of Donald Trump bragging about sexually assaulting women, and laughing about it. I think of the women I know, friends, who are bring re-traumatized, victimized all over again; and the Christian leaders who are defending Donald Trump—"locker-room talk," they call it; and my own growing conviction that if this is Christianity, if they are Christian, then I can't be. They are not my tribe. And I think of the devastation of Hurricane Matthew this past weekend and the impossibility of making sense of it, though some will try. I think, *Perhaps I need another line of work if the job of Christians these days is to defend harassers and explain hurricanes.*

And then a prayer, a few words from a psalm come to me, an anchor, a still point in the midst of the swirling: "Return to your rest, O my soul, for the Lord has dealt bountifully with you."

Then I notice, once more, the scurrying of a squirrel, the rippling of the pond's surface, and the sun pulling back the scrim. Mindfulness is back; I'm back.

On Oak Forest: I crest a small hill and—this hasn't happened before—I don't see the path forward. I can't see it. No brush, weeds, or growth delineate the path, mark its borders. There are only dead, fallen leaves.

This is what midlife can feel like for some—and quite suddenly. We say, "I've never seen it like this before, never been here before."

> And I remember what Quakers say: Way will open.
> I'm asking: What is the way forward for my faith?
> I'm asking: What will it look like when it settles again?

On Spring Hollow: I stop on the bridge to watch the creek, so clear I can see the bed, just a few ripples as the water slides between rocks, purls over them, but it's calm enough to mirror the sky, a reflection of yellow-white-pink clouds announcing the sunset behind me. As I gaze through the water, I touch my deepest longing: to be transparent to God and at rest in myself, satisfied with what love—God's love—has made me—is making me—letting go of all else. If way opens for this longing's fulfillment, if my faith settles here, that will be enough. "Give me nothing more than your love and grace," Ignatius wrote. "These alone are enough for me."

On the way back to the car: a gnatcatcher I can't identify perched in a tree—its needlelike beak, its stillness, its waiting, its mindfulness.

— TRAIL ELEVEN —

Heeding the Call of Community

Christian community is not an ideal we have to realize, but rather a reality created by God in Christ in which we may participate.

–Dietrich Bonhoeffer

Friendship, marriage, family, religious life, and every other form of community is solitude greeting solitude, spirit speaking to spirit, and heart calling to heart. . . . Thus all forms for life together can become ways to reveal to each other the real presence of God in our midst.

–Henri Nouwen

WALK 31

Springing from Solitude

Today reminds me of the first warm day in spring, when neighbors emerge from hibernation, shake hands, delight in the daffodils peeking out of the ground, and ask each other what they did for Thanksgiving, since they haven't seen one another since then. Today is like that because it's seventy-five degrees in the middle of October, after two cold weeks and the season's first frost. The specter of winter haunts us, rattles its chains at the door, threatening us with frigid isolation, yet something calls us from our homes. A deep instinct to connect rises in us, urges us to our cars, until we are here, gathered like worshipers on a Sunday to fill the grand cathedral of creation, giving the lie to our individualism, thumbing our noses at the myth that we can make it on our own. "Community springs forth from solitude," Henri Nouwen writes, "and without a community, communion with God is impossible."

Maybe that instinct brought these parents along with the kid who shouts, "A snake!" loud enough that I rush over. I was just thinking in the car that I have yet to see a snake here. The family doesn't seem to mind I've joined their pod. Though I miss the snake, I do see a ruby-crowned kinglet, dancing above our heads. I wonder if he wants to see the snake too.

Maybe the instinct to connect lured this young couple here, goofing around on the playground, she in a white tank-top, black leggings, with a sweatshirt tied around her waist, and he carrying a backpack for the two of them. She climbs the rope ladder into the playhouse, calling her partner a party-pooper for not joining her. I hear giggles as she climbs back down and gets twisted in the ladder, then the man's solicitous, "Are you hurt?"

Maybe the hope of community drew the gang behind me, puzzled about whether a bird is a red-headed or a red-bellied woodpecker. (*If they had ever seen a red-headed one, they wouldn't be confused*, I think). They walk to the pond and see a small snake skimming the surface. An older couple near the pond tells them, "You guys picked a good day." A woman with a fanny pack says, eyeing the serpent, "You don't see that every day." A turtle swims in the opposite direction of the snake, surfacing slowly, like a submarine.

And maybe it's the need for connection that carried this woman here with her friend. A tan, older woman, she wears khaki pants, sandals with tight support socks, and an unbuttoned plaid shirt with a t-shirt underneath. I'm guessing she's in her sixties.

"I'll just grab this young man's staff," she jokes to her friend, as she reaches for my walking stick. "I left my cane at the house and my knees are bad, but I'm *going* to have my walk," she tells me, determination in her voice.

"It's beautiful out," her friend says. "See how the ducks are taking a bath?"

"Well, they're enjoying this warm day as much as we are—so are all these people," the sandaled woman says. "There are lots of people here because it's a Saturday," she says to me. "I used to come here on weekdays, but now I have radiation every day." Only as she says this do I notice her wig and the braces strapped around her wrists.

I wonder why the woman is telling me this. I'm not asking open-ended questions to sustain conversation, as a book I have on how to make friends advises. And since I'm an introvert who often stands around with my arms crossed, a posture that does not invite conversation even from the most gregarious, I assume I'm not emitting tell-me-your-secrets vibes. People on airplanes don't even talk to me, yet she volunteers.

Could it be that her illness has created a sense of alienation, a feeling of distance, and her coming here—walking with a friend, conversing with a stranger—is a strategy to re-connect, to satisfy her need for human community?

In the gospels, Jesus heals many people. As modern readers, we can fixate on the physical healing—the "miracle"—but as one of my students who preached recently in class on Jesus's healing of a woman with a crippling back disease pointed out, when Jesus heals, he also restores marginalized people to community. Even in the twenty-first century, illness still isolates, throws up barriers like a little pig building a house of brick. Perhaps this woman is tired of it, and is taking the initiative to tear them down. Or maybe she can see to the heart of things and knows these barriers are illusions; maybe she's in touch with a deep truth that says we belong together, and she's determined to live it out.

Maybe she sees what Albert Einstein expressed in a quotation I remember being attributed to him: "Our separateness from one another is an optical illusion."

Maybe that's what all of these people see, what all of us know.

Whether we realize it or not.

———

There was a box of trophies and mementos in front of me that had been taking up too much real estate for too long; it was time throw some out. Some decisions were easy. I didn't need to keep fifty prom pictures; one for the photo album would be enough, and that only because it might amuse my kids someday. And I didn't need a paper I wrote for Latin class, with the lowest grade I got in high school marked in red ink on the last page, along with the affirmation that my "content is good as usual," but I had "slipped mechanically" and made other mistakes the teacher "thought had been resolved."

But the tangle of trophies proved a trickier matter. Holding each one, I could feel again the pride of being called to the stage to receive, for instance, the Senior Band Award ("That means I was the best," I told the boys), or the Louis Armstrong Jazz Award ("That means I was the best," I told them), or an academic letter sweater, sagging with more medals and ribbons pinned to it than I could quickly count ("That means I was the best").

Trophies are metaphors for the work of our early stages in life, the work of acquiring competence, even mastery, in certain areas; the work of developing a solid, healthy identity, a sense of self; the work of beginning to sketch an answer to the question, "Who am I?" of discovering yourself as an individual, a unique "I" among a host of "Thous"—all of it necessary, important work, because, as spiritual writer Richard Rohr notes, in the first half of life, we "need to feel 'special'; we need our 'narcissistic fix.'" What we don't realize, until later, is that, as he puts it, "Once you have your narcissistic fix, you have no real need to protect your identity, defend it, prove it, or assert it." In other words, you don't need to keep the trophies.

The downside of this necessary work is the belief that it's a zero-sum game, that for me to have a solid identity, someone else's must be diminished. There is only one senior band award, only one jazz award, only one valedictorian. There is an ineradicable competitiveness in this business of developing a sense of self, of establishing our individuality.

I wasn't the valedictorian in high school, by the way, which I remembered as I held my salutatorian trophy, that word which means, for all practical purposes, "second best," etched on a cheap metal plate glued to the base. Feeling its weight, I remembered the picture of me in the yearbook giving my speech at graduation, a yellow tassel dangling in my face as I leaned toward the microphone. As I wrote my speech—shortly after the beginning of my days of religious fervor and my call to preach—my mom kept hovering, asking nervously, "You're not going to preach to them, are you?" In fact, I did tell them they needed Jesus, but tastefully, I think. The picture in the yearbook, however, had a more neutral caption: "Salutatorian Roger Owens tells his classmates about the importance of religion." I was somebody, an individual—who happened to come in second, just once.

But, to echo Robert Frost's poem, "Mending Wall," something there is that doesn't love competition and the walls it creates, that doesn't love the jockeying for position and power that can generate a narcissistic fix, but can also keep us isolated, prisoners of our own egos.

On the eve of his crucifixion, Jesus prayed a prayer, a *long* one, for his disciples—the ones alive then and all the ones to come after. He prayed that his disciples might be united, just as he and his divine Abba were united. "Holy Father, protect them in your name, so that they may be one, as we are one." He was praying that we might overcome the competitiveness and egocentricity that keeps us disconnected and alone, even if somewhat satisfied with our achievements. He was praying that we might discover among one another the mystery at the heart of his relationship with God: a unity born of mutual love and self-giving, one that does not erase difference, but neither allows differences to become dividing walls. He was praying for all humanity.

Yes, there is something that doesn't like competitive, separate egos duking it out to secure their places in the world, and that something—rather, Someone—is the divine Spirit, who draws, woos, beckons us from our places of seclusion, our hermitages, our self-made identities, that we might find our authentic selves in community—in communion with one another in God.

We can become alert to that divine summons in midlife, when the trophy case is full and we start to wonder what more there is, when we begin to hope that being an individual on top—or not on top, but an individual, nonetheless—will yield to a richer existence, give way to something more genuine and life-giving, something like authentic connection.

I am not surprised that Thomas Merton had his mystical experience when he was forty-three years old. A decade earlier, in 1948, his autobiography, *The Seven Storey Mountain*, was published and became a surprise bestseller. A memoir about escaping the world into the seclusion of the monastery ironically made him world-renowned at the age of thirty-three. He became somebody famous by writing about how we discover who we really are alone with God. He had accomplished the work of early life. But in 1958, on a rare trip outside of the monastery, God showed him there was more:

> In Louisville, at the corner of Fourth and Walnut, in the center of the shopping district, I was suddenly overwhelmed with the realization that I loved all those people, that they were mine and I theirs, that we could not be alien to one another even though we were total strangers. It was like waking from a dream of separateness . . .

His experience was a moment in which Jesus's prayer was answered, when one man was given a vision of a destiny meant for all people and intended to be experienced here and now in the joy of community.

Now I see that God is still answering that prayer, which, since it was offered on the eve of his crucifixion, was Jesus's own valedictory address—a speech in which you say the single most important thing you can say, in which you boil down all the wisdom and insight and knowledge you possess, and utter it as clearly and directly as possible, which Jesus did: *May they be one.*

May they be one. A prayer answered when a monk sees through the illusion of separateness; when a family huddles at a pond with strangers and watches a snake; when a woman with cancer stops you and unveils her heart just a little, and answers questions you never asked, because there's a Spirit who longs to knock down walls.

A prayer answered when you take a bag of trophies, their faux marble corners puncturing the plastic bag, and hoist it into a dumpster, because you have to make some room in your life, a life in its middle, not for mementos of recognitions past, nor for honors yet to come, but room for people: family, friends, and strangers, those potential friends in disguise.

What I Learned from Dwight's Book

Thanks to Dwight, I understand better what was going on last year, when that sadness made its presence known while I was reading Mark's gospel, when it tightened my chest and throat and called for my attention.

I love a lot about the week-long retreats where I'm invited to speak—the time away, the hours of silence, the private room. Last week's retreat was held at a Mennonite retreat center in the Laurel Highlands of western Pennsylvania, the region's chief destination spot for people who want to soak up the splendor of fall foliage. Nature's scenery was, as a travel brochure might put it, picturesque. And, as a Mennonite establishment, each meal featured the famous Mennonite miracle—food at once simple, healthful, and scrumptious. There are reasons I agree to these gigs.

But the best part is the people I teach with. I've been teaching at these retreats for years, and I've always been paired with an older, wiser presenter, someone with more notches on their belt of experience, and I get to imbibe their insights. Last week was no different. Dwight had recently retired from a position as a full professor teaching spirituality at a seminary near Chicago. He wears a white beard for a wizened look. Next to him, my salt-and-pepper goatee looked brown again. The most striking revelations, though, didn't come from Dwight's talks, strewn as they were with nuggets I greedily hoarded, but from a book of his I brought along to read.

About eighteen months ago, I was where I like to be in the early morning—downstairs in my green La-Z-Boy, a prayer shawl, a gift from a participant at a retreat two years earlier, covering my knees. My Bible was open in my lap as I meditated on Scripture—in this case, the story of Jesus healing a "man who had a withered hand" in Mark's gospel. Many mornings my reading is perfunctory. I don't expect ecstasies and transfigurations every time I open Scripture. The experience is more like a relationship in midlife: steady, true, and lacking drama. But this time, those six words, a simple phrase reducing the identity of this man to a condition, burrowed into me: *man who had a withered hand*. As in the *Wizard of Oz*, when Toto pulls back a curtain on the wizard who prefers to stay hidden, those words unveiled the melancholy face of sadness. I knew enough not to rush by it, not to press on, but to interrogate the sadness instead. Or let it interrogate me.

And here's what it said: *Do you identify with this man because you feel alone, like your connections with others have withered, like you have withdrawn, become cut-off from community? Does your life seem shrunken, withered, alone? Here I am, sadness mixed with longing. Notice me.*

I thought of the life I'd left two years earlier, remembered the city where I'd lived for twelve years—where I met and married my wife, where our three children were born, where we had both pastored churches with so many members between them that we couldn't go the grocery store without running into someone whose child we'd baptized. It was the place where we had been students, where clergy colleagues and friends still lived, where I had the same spiritual director for eight years; the place where I belonged; the place I could call home without hesitation. The sadness wore the face of that memory, that place.

That place had been like a body I was part of, and I now I felt like a transplanted organ. It takes time for a body to accept a new organ. I worked to make it happen, to make a good impression at the seminary, on my colleagues. I worked to satisfy a new batch of students each year with my lectures and jokes, and to help my family adjust to a new world—new geography, new social circles, a new accent to understand.

Still, I'd walk into church each Sunday and no one knew me. Someone else was standing up front, wearing the robes. Still, I'd watch as colleagues headed out to share a pint at a Pittsburgh microbrewery on Friday evenings, and I'd drive home. Still, I'd wonder if I would find a new spiritual director who would help me feel welcomed and safe again.

Looking in the mirror, my appendages appeared healthy. Yet I knew what a man with a withered hand looked like: me.

It shouldn't have come as a surprise. Any person within a couple years of such a major life transition would feel the same. With a move to a new house and a new job, along with the work of helping the whole family settle in, the search for belonging, connection, and friendship slides down the list of urgent "to dos," or slips off completely.

There is also the difficulty of making friends in midlife. I recently read an article in the *New York Times* explaining how, once you're past your thirties, the three conditions sociologists say are needed to build deep relationships—"proximity; repeated, unplanned interactions; and a setting that encourages people to let their guard down and confide in each other"—are rarely met. "As people approach midlife, the days of youthful exploration, when life felt like one big blind date, are fading. Schedules compress, priorities change and people often become pickier in what they want in their friends," the article said, adding, "It's time to resign yourself to situational friends: K.O.F.'s (kind of friends)—for now." External conditions—the indeterminacies of transition and the realities of midlife commitments—obstruct the path of connection.

But resign yourself to being withered? Might there be something interior—something to do with the soul—that rebels against such a situation, and longs for more? Dwight helped me see the answer.

I brought Dwight's book to the retreat, a book on spirituality and life transitions, because I thought it might relate to his lectures, and it was relevant to what I've been ruminating on these days. One day, during the silent hour after my talk, I sat outside on a bench in the sun and read. Dwight's talks—on mysticism and St. Teresa of Avila and the journey of the soul and contemplation and apophatic theology—contained some beautiful, heady stuff, and I loved it. But what spoke to me most were two simple words I read in his book that day: achievement and affiliation.

Here's the gist of it. About the time we become adults, our lives are likely to head down one of two trails, marked either "achievement" or "affiliation." Folks traveling the achievement trail invest more of their life energy in accomplishing goals, acquiring power, and establishing autonomy. Along the other path, people tend to pursue a sense of identity rooted in community rather than accomplishments. But as we approach midlife, something changes, Dwight says. "Whichever pathway has not been dominant begins to emerge. An achiever must learn to seek affiliation. Life requires such a balance from us." And I knew which path I'd been walking since I was a teenager—the trophies I recently trashed revealed that.

But Dwight's interpretation of these two words helped me see that it's not just external pressures creating a longing for connection; there's an inner motivation. My middle-aged soul is longing to explore a different road—to spend more time walking the path of affiliation. I want to discover who I am in community, to know and be known, to dwell in friendship.

In a way, these two—achievement and affiliation—are like the biblical figures Jacob and Esau, twins wrestling in the womb of my soul, brothers fighting for a blessing. For much of my life, I've given the blessing to Jacob, as I sought to discover myself through awards, diplomas, and publications, and as I continue to do through research grants, book contracts, and dreams of tenure and promotion. I doubt this brother will ever go away; maybe he shouldn't. But the path of affiliation is now asking me, the way Esau asked his father, "Have you not reserved a blessing for me?" Esau did not get the blessing he wanted; the blessing of the firstborn had been stolen. The Bible says he hated his brother for it.

I know the way of affiliation can emerge in my life, can receive a blessing, can get the attention it cries out for. I know because I remember what happened when I read the story of the man with a withered hand. After calling the man forward, Jesus said to him, "Stretch out your withered hand." I think Jesus might have been speaking the same thing to me: *You don't have to resign yourself to being withered. You were made for connection. This cry in you—this longing—rises from your divine source. You can heed it. You can flourish in life with others. Stretch yourself out. The way is not closed.*

Not even in my forties.

———

That invitation—stretch out—and the new insights I received last week are the reason, later on the retreat, I invited my friend Johnny, whom I rarely see because he lives in Nashville, to join me on a long hike through the hills so we could reconnect. It's why, this morning, I e-mailed two of my faculty colleagues, both fathers of children my kids' ages, and invited them to meet for coffee so that we could find the space to connect over something other than the anxieties about the tenure process or annoyances over difficult students, space somewhere other than the hallway that houses our offices.

And it's why—miracle of miracles—I invited my mother-in-law to join me on my walk this Sunday afternoon. Usually I take her to the library book sale on Sundays when they're visiting, where she buys a trunk full of used cookbooks, swears me to secrecy, and hides them from my father-in-law for as long as she can. But I knew that she, more than anyone, would appreciate this place in the fall.

And I knew, hearing again the call of affiliation, that I didn't want to walk alone.

Though that's what I'm doing, because she and Ginger were out too late last night shopping for Simeon's birthday so he can have presents from his grandparents before they leave, and Sunday afternoon is the perfect time for a replenishing nap.

So I guess I'll just have to describe for her how the yellow leaves from this maple tree are mingling so effortlessly on the ground with the dried leaves of a nearby oak, as if they, too, are seeking affiliation. And I'll have to tell her how, when twenty white-throated sparrows erupt from the brush, I'm reminded that in the winter they flock with dark-eyed juncos, proving false the dictum that "birds of a feather flock together," and showing that creation finds connection in surprising ways, and teaches us how to join in.

I'll have to paint for her a picture with words of the garnet leaves of the oak trees, canopying the pavilion, hanging over the pond, describe how they glow purple in the light of the early evening, how the branches and leaves of three trees have sought affiliation so long they now look connected, intermingled—a trinity of trees producing one great profusion of garnet.

And I'll have to tell her about these eleven mallards resting on a log—which sounds like the beginning of a children's song—who have chosen on this Sunday evening to find themselves in community. And then I'll ask if she'd like to come tomorrow—after her nap.

WALK 33

For All the Saints

Sometimes the best conversations happen in the dark, when the light disappears, and with it the other figures in the room—all the physical messes that distract, and some of the mental diversions that keep us from hearing or speaking the thoughts in our souls. Sometimes our best conversations happen in the dark, when the intimidating gaze of our interlocutor is shrouded, and all we have to do is receive their words and the words we discover inside ourselves. So it was last night, as I was putting Mary Clare to bed.

She asked me to turn out the light and rub her feet, which I did, thinking of Jesus washing the disciples' feet—a gift to them, and a gift to himself, as well. It was a gift to rub her sore feet—soft, smooth, solid six-year-old feet.

"You know, tomorrow is a special day—All Saints' Day," I said. "It's the day we remember and celebrate all the people who have lived and died loving and following God. We call those people saints."

"Were they saints even as children?" I sensed her interest. Of course, she would wonder that. She's a child after all, and God has become of great interest to her. Sometimes I catch her praying before bed, which is not a regular practice in our family, and when she says grace before dinner, she's not content, as the boys are, to recite the simple rote prayer we've been saying for years. She improvises, adds her own gratitudes and petitions.

"Yes," I said, "some were children." I thought of Therese of Lisiseux, cloyingly pious as a child, who discovered her call to be a nun when she was nine and entered the convent six years later, in 1888. And I thought of Catherine of Sienna, the fourteenth-century mystic, who had her first vision of Christ, who was wearing a papal tiara, when she was six, and vowed, when she was seven, to remain a virgin her whole life. I thought of Clare, after whom our Mary Clare is named, who at eighteen—not exactly a child, but unmarried and still under her parents' care—absconded in the night to join St. Francis in a life of voluntary poverty, against her parents' wishes.

And then there's Mary, Jesus's mother, after whom Mary Clare is also named, who was still a child when she said the "yes" on which God relied in order to be with us in the flesh, to be the Emmanuel who God from eternity determined to be. (As I thought about these young women, I wasn't sure how soon I wanted them to become role models for my daughter. *Sneaking away from parents in the middle of the night?* Maybe I should hide their stories a little longer from her impressionable mind.)

"Some people don't recognize God's love and decide to follow him until much later in life," I continued, "but some kids can tell how much God loves them and know they want to follow God's way of love at a very young age."

We said no more, but held this possibility together in the silence, in the dark.

I don't know if she's ever said yes to an angel; the way she likes to talk, chances are good she would have told me. But she often says yes to me when I ask if she'd like to take a walk, though I don't have time to ask this afternoon. When she sees me walk out of the bedroom with my old navy pants, walking shoes, favorite many-pocketed shirt I grabbed off the floor, and staff in hand, she asks if she can come. And, to my surprise, Simeon does too—anything, I guess, to delay homework.

On the way, I ask Mary Clare, "Do you remember what special day it is?"

"Wait. . . . All Saints' Day?"

"Yes."

"Oh, Dad," she says, "I was extra kind to a friend at recess today."

"You were? Why?"

"I want to follow God, and I think God wants me to be kind."

She'd been playing with a hula hoop, when some other girls wanted it, so she let them have it. "Even though I felt a little sad," she adds. As she tells the story, I'm conflicted. Jesus did say to deny yourself in order to follow him, but six seems a little young for that. Self-denial should come after learning to stand up for yourself, it seems to me, after developing a strong enough sense of self that you have something to deny. Maybe it was too much pressure, naming her after Mary, the Mother of God, *and* St. Clare.

When we arrive, one of the first things we notice is the maple tree near the education center, still so full the last time I was here, now half-empty. It's past its peak, and so many of the yellow leaves have fallen—have denied themselves and let go, have drifted down to join the communion of leaves on the ground.

If you only imagine saints in the Protestant way, they have no particular appeal, for Protestants are those people who believe, in theory if not in practice, the words of the bumper sticker, "Christian's aren't better—just forgiven." All Christians are saints, we say. Faith in Jesus and their baptisms makes them that. In his letters, Paul calls all Christians "saints"—"To the saints in Christ Jesus who are in Philippi . . ." He didn't mean a select few in Philippi, or anywhere else—spiritual over-achievers, cream of the Christian crop, an inner saintly circle, the legitimately holier-than-thou. He meant all followers of Jesus, anyone who had taken the plunge.

Sixteenth-century reformer Martin Luther immortalized this view with a pithy slogan when he said that a Christian is *simul iustus et peccator*—at the same time both righteous and a sinner. Righteous, because we've been declared righteous by God on account of Christ's actual righteousness—we get to borrow Christ's right-eousness, so to speak—but sinful because, well, we're actually sinful. The righteous-ness is really Christ's, and God's declaration doesn't change the facts on the ground. After the declaration—"Righteous! Forgiven!"—we're still conflicted, greedy, envi-ous, false selves making a mess of things. Some might say this is one of the few empirically verifiable theological positions, at least the latter half. Just hang out at a church for a while.

This understanding of sainthood means a lot to me, for every year for the past seven years, I have, on All Saints' Day, allowed myself to imagine my Dad, surpris-ingly joined to God—probably more of a surprise to him than to anyone else. And, though he mellowed in his later years, he carried both his virtues and his vices to his death, as all of us will. He was a wonderful man, but he was no saint. *Simul iustus et peccator.*

For instance, on my family's last visit with Dad before he died, several months before Mary Clare was born, I remember him, sitting in his blue leather La-Z-Boy, frustrated by his pneumonia, which had settled into his lungs after a fall cracked a vertebrae, confining him to his chair. Simeon ran into the room, a rambunctious five-year-old at the time, and threw a paper airplane, though he'd been asked by my mom not to do it again. It glided to a stop in my dad's lap. He grabbed it, shouted a few words I don't remember, crumpled the plane in his fists, and threw it at Simeon. Dad's face burned red and his sizeable, eighty-eight-year-old jowls shook in anger.

I knew such impatience was just one line in the sketch of his character, but for Simeon it was the last and most vivid recollection he has of my father, Dad's whole character crushed into one moment like a paper airplane crinkled into a ball.

A few months later, after his death, I sat in worship on parental leave; Mary Clare was a week old. It was All Saints' Sunday. The choir and a small orchestra were performing John Rutter's *Requiem*, and for the first time in a long time there was someone close to me for whom I was praying, "May he rest in peace." And I was giving thanks that people who aren't saints—who take their anger and impatience, their foibles and their hang-ups, to the grave, along with their many virtues; that is, people like my dad—are saints anyway. They get to be numbered among those the book of Revelation describes as robed in white, worshiping God day and night; people who are not better, just forgiven.

Only Dad might be wanting a break from worship to watch the Cubs.

As I hang out in the threshold of midlife, and imagine my own life over the next four or five decades, I'm not satisfied with just being forgiven, however great a gift that is. When I read the stories of the Saints, with a capital "S," I want their kind of life. I want a winsome, beautiful life, a life that stands open to others in love, that sees through and beyond the divisions and distinctions that mar our perceptions of the world, what's now popular to call "dualistic thinking"—us versus them, humanity versus the rest of creation, even life versus death. I want to experience a love that both sees and expresses the unity of all things in the Life that holds all together. That kind of living, I suspect, takes getting better.

Protestants need to relearn the Catholic view of saints, to rediscover the value of holding up men and women throughout the ages whose lives have been open to God, unusually sensitive and responsive to the Holy Sprit's dualism-overcoming work. People who can inspire us—and pray for us—as we grow in holiness, *actual* holiness. People whom the Spirit has made better, like Clare and Therese of Lisieux and Catherine of Sienna. And my favorite: Francis.

At the end of this month, when our family schlepps the Christmas decorations out of the garage and up the stairs, one box will have the Christmas-themed books: Christmas board books we read to the kids when they were babies, like a chewed-up copy of Margaret Wise Brown's *Christmas in the Barn*—her take on the nativity story, with rhymes and rhythms reminiscent of her *Goodnight Moon*—and some Christmas piano music I've been playing for twenty-five years, a few caroling books, and a book called *Home for Christmas*, an anthology of Christmas tales, including one story I reread every year: "Brother Robber."

In that story, Brother Angelo, one of Francis's companions, is decorating the hermitage on Christmas Eve when three robbers burst in and ask for food. Brother Angelo condemns the robbers for their evil mischief and sends them away. Later that night, Francis returns, and Brother Angelo tells him what happened.

"You said you sent them away?"

"Their hands were red with blood."

"They stretched them out for help and you left them unfilled?"

"They were robbers, Brother Francis."

"They were brothers, Brother Angelo."

Even as I recall this scene, I feel the pull of Francis's love that sees through superficial pigeon-holing, the kind of pigeon-holing most of us use to get through life, to interpret our experience and make it in the world—and I want to get better. I want the kind of love that glimpses below the surface to a deeper communion, a love that knows that robbers are brothers, that non-human creatures are also children of the Creator, as Francis tries to teach us in his "Canticle of Creation," where he names the elements of the earth as siblings with us in a universal family. I want to learn that even death—when one's trust is in the Love that was there before anything else and will be without end—can be called a sister.

When your life has been so transfigured by that kind of love, they don't call you just Francis, anymore, not even Brother Francis. They call you *Saint*.

Saints—they remind us we're forgiven. And by helping us to see the world as we've never seen it before, they give us hope that we, too, can get *better*.

Heading down Goldenrod, I tell Mary Clare that I often think of Francis on these walks. It's the noisy, incessant chatter of birds that makes me think of the medieval fool for God, that and Mary Clare's own continued chatter about the saints. Francis felt a kinship with the rest of creation, so much so that he preached to the chicka-dees, I tell her, as two of those tiny creatures, black-hooded like medieval knights, twitter in the branches above us, as if we are all part of one company, traveling together.

"Did they understand him?" she asks.

I give some explanation about how, because Francis was one of God's special friends, and because all of creation is in God, maybe they did. She raises her eyebrows and nods, as if this makes perfect sense to her, as if she's thinking about what she might want to say to the chickadees, what good news or moral advice she has to offer. But instead, she asks another question.

"Isn't it sad that we don't ever thank God for all of creation?" Her eyebrows are still raised, a cowlick on the end of her right one pointing the hairs perpetually upward. The reflected light from her sequined rainbow-swirl shirt glows red on her face.

Simeon, feeling less inclined to be quizzical about saints, has walked ahead of us to the pond, where he sees a great blue heron. "Hurry up—a heron," he shout-whispers, hoping we'll hear him, and the heron won't. We scramble to reach him, and the three of us huddle together, mesmerized by this bird, towering in the shallow water, jabbing its deadly lance-of-a-beak into the pond to stab fish. We marvel at its persistence after each miss, at the way it walks on spindly legs, the way it stealthily stalks its prey, the way it embodies the unity of the circle of life—it lives, fed by death, like the rest of us.

"We could thank God for creation right now," I say, surprised at my own suggestion.

"Yes, let's do," Mary Clare says.

And so I pray as the three of us keep our eyes open, watching the bird.

"Dear God, thank you for heron, for his elegance and grace and fierce beauty, for what he teaches us about how you care for your creation, how you give each thing you've made what it needs. Thank you that he is being himself, doing what you created him to do, and that we get to watch, amazed. Amen."

Or thank you for *brother* heron, I should have said.

We stare in silence for another minute before moving on. I walk away genuinely grateful, grateful that my midlife longing for community—for connection, for friendship—seems to reflect the order of things, to mirror a mysterious truth the saints teach us, one at midlife I am eager to learn: that we are already part of a community more magnificent than we can imagine, joined to brothers and sisters and neighbors near and far, to poor and rich, weak and strong, to human beings with backgrounds, histories, and cultures that make us think we are so different. And that we are connected to a family that includes chickadees and herons—a reunion each time I'm here.

Yes, my longing for connection ascends in me from a deep place, like magma from the core of my being rising through fissures in my soul. But it rises from a deeper place still—even from the heart of the Divine Community of Love.

WALK 34

All in One

"You can only stare at one tree for so long." That's the assessment of an eleven-year-old, ready to go home. It's also debatable.

He's here because he was sad he missed the heron we saw on our last walk, when he stayed home. But we haven't seen the heron today, or much else for that matter: a few birds at the feeder by the gift shop; the maple tree we saw last time still half full of leaves, now with only five or six holding on; a toddler, first disturbing the peace at the pavilion and later tumbling around the playground like a puppy released into the yard for the first time. Mary Clare brought my mother-of-pearl opera glasses, but hasn't had a good reason to use them.

Until now.

As we walk past the playground and the tumbling toddler, following the wooden fence to our right that separates the path from the meadow, a vision beckons us to stop: a lone tree in the middle of the meadow, the one birds rest in on their trek over the meadow, the one I've watched cedar waxwings spring from to catch insects midair, the one I've seen indigo buntings perch atop like blue beacons. But I've always been looking at the birds, never at the tree itself. Now I see the tree, still playing its part in the season's concert, like the final violins in Haydn's "Farewell" Symphony, bowing away after all the other musicians have left the stage. This tree—full, fiery yellow, a sun refusing to set.

I feel like we should remove our shoes, but I'm glad we don't as Mary Clare climbs onto the rough wooden fence—despite her brother's warning that she could fall and injure her head—and balances precariously, training her opera glasses on the tree.

I observe the tree without using my binoculars because I'm not interested in focusing on its leafy splendor alone. I want to see it in context, ponder it within its place in the web of creation—meadow around it, hill rising behind, pond in the distance, sky above, sun looking down and adding heat to the fire. This tree—the focal point on creation's broad canvas.

"I'm ready to go," Silas says.

"But I'm still looking at this tree."

"You can only stare at one tree for so long."

As he says this, I think of something German theologian Dietrich Bonhoeffer said. People will complain, he said, when whole chapters of Scripture are read in public worship, whining it's too hard to follow, too complicated. He responds to these imagined complainers, writing that "every Scripture reading will be 'too long,' even the shortest." One phrase, a single word, is too long because each word contains the whole. "The Scripture is a complex unity, and every word, every sentence, contains such a diversity of relationships to the whole that it is impossible to keep track of the whole when listening to individual portions of it." If you told Bonhoeffer you can only contemplate one word of Scripture for so long, I suspect he would reply, "Really?"

Isn't the phenomenon the same with what the Celtic Christians viewed as the book of creation? They knew the mystery of the connection of all things, the impossibly possible diversity of relationships within the natural world. And how much more should we, the beneficiaries of twenty-first century science, know this to be true? The history of the universe can be read in one tree, a tree that contains traces of the Big Bang, the intricate interdependence of all that is written in crevices of bark, in veins of translucent leaves. To read that tree is to read the history of creation and life, from the trees in the Garden of Eden to the tree of life in the New Jerusalem. This tree is one word from God echoing all others, one note in the concerto of creation resonating with all the rest.

If it's true of one word of Scripture, and true of one word of Creation, then maybe it's true of the word of this life of mine I've been meditating on all these months, considering on these many walks. Some might see my midlife project as narcissistic and fear that I might disappear into my own navel if I gaze at it too intently. "You can only look at one life for so long," they might say—which I wouldn't deny if I believed humans were isolated individuals, hermetically sealed souls roaming the world, as Western Enlightenment thinkers would have liked us to believe. But we're not. We exist in a infinite nexus of relationships. Christian theology goes even further. The more you attend to your life, the more you penetrate the mystery of your humanity with ever sharpening awareness, the more likely you are to experience the "honor [it] is to be a cell in the Cosmic Body of Christ," as Louis Savary writes. A cell, I would add, with permeable membranes.

My life no less tells the story of the universe and the history of the stars, the intercommunion of all creation, than does this tree, all aglow. The longer I look at my one, wild life—daughter and son beside me, brother sun above and sister moon hiding in the sky, mother earth beneath my feet and cousin tree across the way—the wider I see the nexus of relationships that stretches in all directions, into an infinity of yesterdays and just as many tomorrows, even into the heart of the Incomprehensible One we call God, Mystery, Love.

Maybe we should take off our shoes not just before burning bushes and flaming fall trees, but before one another as well.

"You can only stare at one tree for so long."

Really?

— TRAIL TWELVE —

Experiencing God, Following God

But the light fades, the will weakens, the humdrum returns. . . .
But the Eternal Inward Light does not die when ecstasy dies, nor
exist only intermittently, with the flickering of our psychic states.
Continuously renewed immediacy, not receding memory of the
Divine Touch, lies at the base of religious living.

–Thomas Kelly

WALK 35

God and Beer

Basil-infused oil from my Italian sub dribbles down my hand, onto my shirt. Before I came here, I dropped half of my sandwich off with Ginger, who's preparing Advent decorations this afternoon at the church where she works. To the left of the bench where I'm sitting, water drips from a tube rigged-up by a naturalist. Cardinals dance noisily in and around the shallow puddle.

I left Philadelphia at 6:20 this morning, where I spent almost a week in the archives of Haverford College studying the papers of Quaker mystic Thomas Kelly, author of the spiritual classic *A Testament of Devotion*. After several full days in a library, it's good to eat a spicy sub outside and to gaze across what I now think of as my meadow.

After throwing away my trash and going to the restroom, I begin my walk. The leaves are so deep some places along the trail that, when I kick my feet, I'm reminded of walking through the surf on a beach, the kind that makes your thighs ache later. The oak leaves are shiny, thick, dark brown, like polished shoe leather. The maple leaves are a lighter brown, yellowish and delicate, like the brittle manuscripts of Kelly's I read this week. Some of the sermons I handled were almost a hundred years old, the back pages listing in Kelly's elegant script the dates and places he'd preached them as he itinerated in the 1920s.

One manuscript I studied was a lecture he'd given in the mid-1930s, "What Is the Mystic's Experience?" In it he distinguishes between two kinds of mystical experience, the first of which he labels "mild." Some might not even call them mystical, these gentle touches of awe and wonder that any number of encounters can elicit. I think he must be speaking autobiographically when he talks about how the beauty of a mathematical equation can trigger a mild mystical experience—that's never happened to me. But he also notes how nature can convey one into an experience of what Rudolf Otto called the numinous, the *mysterium tremendum et fascinans*—that mystery that is both frightening and enthralling. And these are not always so mild.

Reading that lecture, I remembered how surprised I was two years ago, when my family visited Niagara Falls for the first time. I expected the typical tourist experience, not the religious one I received. As we walked along the river toward the falls, I admired the roaring rush of water tumbling vigorously over rocks as it churned powerfully, inexorably forward. But I didn't expect to be overwhelmed by the thunderous display of might, by the terrifying energy of the water crashing down, of the cataract. Tears mingled with the mist dampening my face, and I started spontaneously singing the hymn "How Great Thou Art."

Then I thought, *Who are you, and what have you done with Roger?* Now I wonder if Kelly would have called this a mild mystical experience.

He also spoke of "acute" mystical experiences, some rapturous, as in the case of Teresa of Avila, some dissolving a sense of self in an experience of profound union with God, like Meister Eckhart's. There's no evidence Kelly had had any such experiences before he gave this lecture, but just a few years later he would be, as he put it in a letter to his wife, "shaken by the experience of Presence . . . laid hold on by a Power, a gentle, loving, but awful Power." He would be met by that *mysterium tremendum et fascinans.*

It's hard for me to believe that just a year ago I sat across from Sister Anna and struggled to answer questions about how I experience God. I think I had hoped she might be able to fix the situation, but instead she's helped me see the situation needs no fixing. I don't want to spend the rest of my life chasing experiences of God, mystical bliss. I know a life of love—of faithfulness, service, self-gift—can't be sustained by extraordinary experiences alone, even if they come.

Just as I've wrestled with the reality, over these walks, that my images of God are not God—a reality that, as a theologian, I somehow knew to be true, but had yet to allow to sink into the cells of my being—so now I'm recognizing a concomitant truth: my experiences of God, such as they are, are not God, either. It would be foolish of me to arrange the second half of my life—structure my time, invest my energy, devote my material resources—toward the pursuit of an experience that's not God. As Thomas Merton said, "The experimental 'awareness' of the presence of God is just as truly a created thing as a glass of beer." And I don't even like beer.

A friend's spiritual director asked her recently, "Do you want the consolations of God, or the God of consolations?"

Okay, consolations are nice, I admit it, and even if I don't chase them, I won't refuse such an experience if it comes, won't deny the Giver by rejecting the gift. No, I'll stop when awe strikes, I'll give thanks when I encounter the numinous (if I know it), and I'll bask in a sense of inner peace should it arrive.

Which it does right now, as peacefully as the sky begins to rain leaves down upon me, a gentle breeze dislodging them above; as gently as they swirl around me, as if I'm in a snow globe after the shaking has stopped and the snowflakes begin to settle—leaf-flakes settling all around me and a mild awe arising within me and the tune of an old hymn, last sung at Niagara Falls, slipping through my lips.

WALK 36

Christk the King

I don't know if my running into this sign is itself a sign from God—a warning, perhaps—or just a coincidence. But it says what I need to hear.

It's November 20, the last Sunday of the year on the Christian liturgical calendar; Christ the King Sunday. We read from the book of Colossians this morning,

> He is the image of the invisible God, the firstborn of all creation; for in him all things in heaven and on earth were created, things visible and invisible, whether thrones or dominions or rulers or powers. . . . He is the head of the body, the church; he is the beginning, the firstborn from the dead, so that he might come to have first place in everything.

The verses depict the glory and authority of the risen Christ.

The invisible God: God beyond all images, metaphors, beyond all description. Except, Christianity teaches that humanity has been given one true picture of God: Jesus. God does have a face. There is an image of God that captures the truth; there is one embodied life of humility and divine servanthood to which we can look. Today the church announces through its Scriptures and songs and sermons that God has exalted and made this humble servant king. God only wears one crown, and it's no longer a crown of thorns. It's the crown of a king, reigning in glory.

An outdated metaphor, if not positively misleading, I think, as I make footprints in the first snow of the year. The ground is still too warm for measurable accumulation, but flakes cling to each blade of grass and frost the layer of leaves, so that the ground in some places has two blankets, leaves and snow. The first day of snow. The first day for me to wear gloves since last winter. The first day to pull the flaps of my cap down over my ears, the way I did on that first walk almost eleven months ago. And I do it on this last Sunday of the Christian year, the Sunday of Christ the King—another image, like "God is in charge," that's losing its grip on me.

Not that I don't appreciate the sentiment. Christ the King Sunday is a relative newcomer to the church year, established in 1925 when the world was still repairing itself from the aftermath of the Great War. It was meant to remind us that in a world of presidents and potentates, some more benign than others, all earthly rulers are relativized by the One True Sovereign: the Christ, whom God raised from the dead and seated on the divine throne in a heavenly coronation, making the earth his footstool—as if God had been reading the script from Psalm 110, "The LORD said to my lord, 'Sit at my right hand until I make your enemies your footstool.'"

And we need the reminder today, just a few weeks after Americans elected Donald Trump president, a man completely too eager to be in charge. For Christians who voted for him, imagining him to be a kind of messiah who will bring evangelical Christians back to power in this country and favor "Christian" moral principles, even if he flouts them personally, and for Clinton supporters, like me, who are still wallowing in despair and staggering disbelief, this Sunday can—but won't—be a moment of recalibration: from God's perspective, there is only one King; all others are mere crossing guards.

But here's the problem. Calling Christ "King" assumes we know what we are talking about, as if there were a class of people called kings—emperors, czars, caesars, monarchs, shoguns, presidents—with Jesus on top as the bigwig, the head honcho, the King of kings and Lord of lords, as if to say these earthly kings think they are in charge, and always have thought so, but Christ is the one who rules. I suspect that's what most Christians thought this morning when we sang about thrones and crowns and royal diadems. And I thought, *Really? He's one of those, just bigger?*

I'm still thinking that this afternoon, which after the change to standard time already feels like evening, as the shadows lengthen and the breeze, emboldened by the sun's setting, chaps my face, urging me to turn around. It's what I am thinking about as I turn left off of Spring Hollow and onto Meadowview. It's what I'm thinking about when, after I walk a few yards, I see a sawhorse blocking the entrance to the Woodland trail, a laminated sign stapled to it and stamped with the Audubon seal, a sign that says more to me than the grounds superintendent who posted it intended: "This trail is CLOSED for hunting season. For your safety, please make use of our other trails during this season."

Some paths are just closed, and it would be foolish to keep trying to follow them. It's not safe to circumvent the barricade. Find a different path.

For your safety, make use of our other trails.

What happens in midlife when our favorite, familiar paths close? Do we heed the warning to try another trail?

Certainly, paths of faith, ways to God, can become closed. Patterns of prayer and devotion that once made us feel close to God, connected, can become blocked, for whatever reason, and we wake up one morning, and the feeling has vanished; the sense of Presence is gone. We try what worked yesterday, and it doesn't work today. Something has changed. John of the Cross called this a dark night of the soul, when those consoling ways of prayer and comforting images of God, the ones that used to give a sense of security and stability—like Christ as King, perhaps—feel stripped away. A barricade appears informing us that the trail is blocked and warns to go another way.

The temptation when that happens? Say, "No." View the barricade as a hurdle to be jumped. Refuse to accept the new reality. After all, how can we be sure there are other paths? We better keep stomping down this one, safety warnings be damned.

Another path that can become obstructed is the path back to a sense of youthful limitlessness, to a time when anything seemed possible, when the future was a blank slate on which we could chalk anything we wanted, then erase and begin afresh, indefinitely. Now at midlife, when we have little choice but to confront our creaturely limits and acknowledge that we are finite beings in time and space, we might search for the trailhead back to our youth and run down it, heedless of the warning, "Closed! Not Safe!"

The fact is the slate was never blank, the horizon never limitless. We *are* creatures, after all, and midlife can be a time to learn how to live well within our human limits. "Being a creature is in danger of becoming a lost art," theologian Rowan Williams said, and midlife presents an opportunity to relish in our creatureliness. But only if we obey the sign warning us not to venture back down the path from which we came.

For your safety, the sign says, *try another trail.*

But there's a challenge. At the nature reserve, there are plenty of trails still open, and I can look at the map or revert to habit, and take a path of my choosing, one that will lead me where I want to go. But if we are willing to turn our backs on the paths that God, or chance, or human limits, or our own decisions, or some inscrutable combination of the four have barricaded, acknowledging that, for our own safety now and flourishing in the future, it's wise not to keep pressing along these paths, what guarantee do we have that we will not see another dead end when we turn? How do we know another path waits to be walked? What if this dead end really *is* the end? Life isn't a nature reserve.

——

The Woodland trail closed, I turn around. The wind blows at my back now, impelling me forward. But I stop, rest my hand on my staff, watch the snow fall, and continue to consider Christ the King. This whole business of Christ being made King, his exaltation, occurs after Christ's condescension, after his human wanderings and agonizing death, about which Paul wrote in the hymn in Philippians 2, which ends, "Therefore, God highly exalted him, and gave him the name that is above every name." Coronation, he's saying, only follows Cross.

As the fingers on my right hand grow numb and I start walking again, the staff in my left hand, my right hand in my jacket pocket, I realize my work is to plumb this image before tossing it out. Maybe hidden in this blocked image is the entrance to another trail.

Christ's tomb—that seemed like a dead end, the way out closed more definitively than any blocked trail at a nature reserve. And yet it wasn't. And on the evening of the Resurrection, the disciples cowered in the locked upper room, their future, for all practical purposes, barricaded closed. They, too, were at a dead end. But it wasn't.

After the Resurrection, not sure what to do next, Peter and the others went back down the path they'd left behind; they went fishing. They couldn't imagine a way forward for themselves. They wondered if their three-year-long journey with Jesus had been a dream. It hadn't been.

I think of Stephen, the church's first martyr, who, just before he was stoned to death, saw a vision of Christ, exalted in glory at God's right hand—a vision of Christ the King. And while he was being stoned, he offered forgiveness for his persecutors. Stephen was literally at a dead end, and he acted as if a way were opening, not closing, a possibility the writer of Acts tried to communicate by showing a picture of Christ as King.

These stories make me think that the exaltation of Christ who was crucified— this pierced servant sitting on a throne and wearing a crown and waving a royal diadem—might not be saying that he is more kingly than all the kings of the earth, that he is more imperial than an emperor, more presidential than a president, more sovereign than a sovereign, more trumpy than a Trump. No. Perhaps it's a way of saying, when God raises to victory the one who faced, suffered under, and defeated the barrier called death, then, for this One to be King in glory at God's right hand, means that he is the guarantor-in-chief, the one who promises that there are always new possibilities, ever new paths, that no end is a dead one forever, that God's infinite creativity is always at work in our lives in the places that seem closed off.

And so we don't need to break through the barricades, either to childhood faith or youthful limitlessness, because wherever we are, in our reality right *now*, the One who found his way out of death is here, with us, promising that other paths are possible.

Not the ones we used to travel.

Not the ones that we can imagine.

And maybe not the ones we would choose.

But other paths are possible, paths that lead to life.

As I head back to the car, I'm picturing the children this morning, circled on the floor around one of our ministers for the children's sermon, just a few feet in front of the altar. Mary Clare was among them, as usual, ready to raise her hand and answer a question. The first question was easy.

"Can someone tell me what this is?" the minster asked, as he displayed a cardboard crown from Burger King.

"A crown!" some kids shouted, while others, more composed, raised their hands.

"Who is in charge?" he asked them—and they knew the answer was Jesus, but they played along. "Who should we put this crown on to remember who's in charge?"

He put it on his own head, but a kid knocked it off. He placed it on a small boy's head, but others snatched it away. And then he stood and put the burnished gold crown, painted with jewels and advertising hamburgers, onto the altar.

"This crown belongs to Christ. He is in charge. He is ruler. He is sitting on the throne. Nothing can change that."

And now I think I know what that might mean, though I wouldn't choose those words, and it's a meaning I will cling to here in the threshold of midlife: there is a divine creativity at work, a divine guarantor, who knows what it's like to face a dead end and yet found a new way to life, one who promises that no blocked path is the final one, that no matter what, there will always be a way forward.

If it takes singing about a crown and throne and scepter to remember that, well, I guess that's alright.

WALK 37

Waning Light

Simeon and I spiraled on the Christmas tree lights before the family hung the two boxes of ornaments Ginger and I have accumulated over fourteen years of marriage, and a few from my life before marriage. I was glad for these miniature bulbs, now that Pittsburgh has entered its season of waning light. Starting about October, whenever I see the sun out, I say, "Better go outside and enjoy the sun—this could be its last appearance until April." Winter in Pittsburgh makes you jealous of Seattle and London.

Atop and around the colored lights, we dangled the ornaments. Simeon argued for purging some of them, claiming they made the tree look junky, "homemade," in his words. He's the family member with the most refined aesthetic sensibilities, and it has bothered him for a few years that our tree looks like a flea market. In the end, I agreed that he could excommunicate the four most egregious from the community of ornaments, including a paper-plate wreath with a photo of Silas in the middle and a snapshot of Simeon in a tongue-depressor frame. Still in our pajamas, we hung the rest, an Anne Murray CD accompanying us with standard Christmas songs, and some not-so-standard, like "Christmas in Killarney." In the end, even with four fewer ornaments, our plastic pine still looked like it was wearing a yard sale.

Decorating completed, we sat in front of the tree, the lights scattering rainbows on the ceiling, and we ate the Christmas cake Simeon had baked the night before: a chocolate Bundt cake, with red-and-white swirled icing dripping down the sides and crushed candy canes studding the top. It was the day before the first Sunday of Advent, and we were ready for the season of light.

Afterwards, Ginger and Simeon went shopping, and I tried to nap in the chair, exhausted from the minimal exertion of decorating. At three o'clock, when they returned, Ginger handed me a bag.

"Merry Christmas early. I got one for myself, too. They were forty percent off."

When I looked inside, I thought, *Is it that obvious?* In the bag was a sun-mimicking lamp, "full-spectrum light, to help conquer the winter blues and restore energy." When I saw it, I remembered my roommate in college, remembered the day mid-fall when he turned to me, wearing a grave expression.

"I need to warn you," he said. "If you find me acting depressed in the coming months, it's because I suffer from light deficiency syndrome."

Having not yet taken Introduction to Psychology, nor having developed a spirit of empathy in my eighteen years of living, I did what I knew even in the moment I shouldn't have done: I laughed. That's a thing? *For real?*

Now, after three winters in Pittsburgh, I think, *I'm sorry, so, so sorry, old friend. Now I understand.*

The sun sets sooner. The gray clouds bustle in. The cold isolates. And anxiety, sadness, listlessness increase. That's why I decided to get dressed and go for a walk. Surely cloud-filtered light is better than none at all.

When I was at Haverford College a couple of weeks ago, researching the papers of Thomas Kelly, I sat in the reading room of the archives by day, studying and photographing his unpublished papers. By night I sat in my guest room at Pendle Hill, a Quaker retreat center, rereading his one book of spiritual literature, *A Testament of Devotion*, published shortly after his death in 1941. The green hardbound book I held was originally purchased by Mrs. T. S. Morris in 1955. The underlines in pencil, blue, and red ink betrayed the many times I'd read it. It never fails to speak to me, and it didn't fail that night.

Kelly begins by painting a picture of the triumphant experience of the Divine Light within each one of us, drawing us to God, transfiguring our daily lives, casting "new glories upon the faces of men." He offers a dramatic yet winsome portrait of a soul wooed by God toward complete commitment, lured by powerful inner experiences of the light of God.

And then he writes, "But the light fades." The inner ecstasy diminishes, sometimes vanishes completely, pales like blue Pittsburgh skies in winter. "Can we stay this fading?" Kelly asks. And we might ask the same thing, as the light of spiritual experience begins to fade in our own lives, as the experience of God wears less vivid shades, especially in midlife as so many other concerns vie for what little mental space we have. Kelly answers that we shouldn't try to hold on to the experience of light because the *presence* of the Divine Light doesn't leave. God's presence is not dependent on "the flickering of our psychic states."

As I reread his words, I thought of Mother Teresa and the scandal caused by the publication of her letters to her spiritual director, portraying her inner life as a spiritual wasteland, a desert, for most of her years. Yet somehow this woman carried on, kept seeing Christ in the poor, continued inspiring a world with generosity and kindness and love. If anyone knew that the light dims, Mother Teresa did, and yet now she is called a saint.

Kelly responds to the fading of the light by encouraging discipline, because though the ecstasy of inner experience will abate—if one ever has such ecstasy—the Light, which is the presence of Christ, remains. And through a life of prayer—chosen and intentional—we can, he suggests, orient ourselves to the God within. We can engage in "internal practices and habits of the mind . . . secret habits of unceasing orientation of the deeps of our being about the Inward Light, ways of conducting our inward life so that we are perpetually bowed in worship, while we are also very busy in the world of daily affairs." Whenever I read this, I wonder, *Is this possible? Even for me?* And this time I added, *Even in midlife?*

He uses a word I don't much like: habit. Habit feels like effort—trying, doing-it-myself—and I've thought of God as the primary agent of the spiritual life. I've been learning that my job is to consent to God's work in my life. But as I sat in that tiny guest room, I looked up across the wooden desk and outside. It was dark, and I realized between now and old age, if I'm blessed to live that long, will be many days and months and years, and maybe Kelly is right, and some of them might be dark. Maybe, if I want to live those years oriented to God, open to God, consenting to all that the refining fires of divine Love want to accomplish in me, my turning to God must become habit, something I choose. I can't wait around for a feeling.

Earlier that day, going through Kelly's papers, I read a tantalizingly vague reference in a letter he wrote to a woman at Yale University. She had invited him to come to Yale to speak on mysticism—that form of religious experience associated with assent to God's work, to God's complete overwhelming the senses and the soul. The manuscript of the talk he gave does not still exist, but in his letter he hints at the topic he wanted to explore:

> I think it would be well not only to talk about the mystic's experience, and the practice of the presence of God, but also to discuss the relation of the sense of Presence to the *will*. I feel definitely that the significant factor in religion is a permanent attitude of will, rather than a less permanent, more variable state of exaltation.

When I want God to pull me to God's very self, want God to deliver consolations that will fuel my journey toward love, want God to pull back the curtain of clouds when they haze my soul, and drench me in divine light, maybe God says, *I've already done all that. I'm here. The light shines in you whether you see it or not. I am saying yes to you in love. And I'm empowering your will to say yes to me. In each moment. Won't you do that?*

The light is fading, but I keep walking in the filtered afternoon light that presses through the screen of clouds. The path is muddy, slippery, and I make dexterous use of my staff so my rear won't meet the ground. A tree has fallen on the path and shattered. I dance gingerly through the tree-limb shards. Leaves float over half the pond, like a quilt turned down on a bed. The uncovered half reflects the trees and the sky, gray, I notice for the first time, with cracks of blue. Seventeen crows fly overhead; their reflection in the now-rippling pond makes them look like demons erupting from a lair.

Fifty yards along Violet, and I encounter a stretch that's perpetually muddy. I usually have to walk several feet off the path to avoid the mud, scraping through bushes and avoiding thorns. But today I find a pleasant surprise. Someone has placed a ten-foot four-by-four across the mud, like the balance beam on my elementary school playground, except this one moves precariously with the mud. Glued to the beam is a strip of black sandpaper to help prevent slipping. I step on the unbalanced beam, put one foot in front of the other, roll each step from heel to toe like a Buddhist monk on a walking meditation. My staff, in the mud, helps to steady me. A thorn bush, reaching over the path, snags my jacket and tries to slow me down, or pull me off, but I keep going and step off the other end onto firm ground.

A permanent attitude of will. Does that mean keep walking, keep stepping forward, keep showing up? It's an attitude of will that has gotten me through almost thirty-seven walks in this year after I turned forty. It's an attitude of will that put one foot in front of another on this bridge that some mysterious gift-giver placed on the path. It's an attitude of will that gets me to my La-Z-Boy earlier than I'd like on most mornings, because I believe God will meet me there—God is already there—and God invites me to show up.

And it's an attitude of will that keeps me showing up, even when I doubt whether God is there, which I'm doing less frequently; even when I didn't "experience" God the day before, or the day before that, or the day before the day before that—which is more likely than not believing. Because God has awakened in me a desire, a longing that, I'm coming to see, can only be filled by God's very presence. There's nothing to make me think all my minutes and hours and days and years of faith won't continue this way: with a God-inspired desire for God, joined with a God-freed will, stepping, ever stepping forward, sometimes in the light, sometimes in the dark, and sometimes in the gray twilight that hovers between.

Advent begins tomorrow, and just as Jewish people light candles throughout Hanukah to remember a light that never went out, Christians will light one each week to remember the coming of the one whom we call the Light of the World, whom the angel told Joseph would be called Emmanuel, God with us—in other words, the Light within.

As I head back to the car, the evening is defying the conventions of the season—it's lighter out now than it was when I left home, the clouds having given way to an evening blue. And I'm remembering another time Jesus promised to be with us, and three tantalizing words in Scripture that one could build a midlife faith upon.

After the resurrection account in Matthew's gospel, Jesus commissioned his disciples. The Bible says the eleven disciples met Jesus on a mountain, and "when they saw him, they worshiped; but some doubted." Three words: *but some doubted.*

These disciples had followed Jesus for three years. They had whined to him, partied with him, misunderstood him, heard his stories, witnessed his miracles and performed their own in his name. These were the same disciples who were told by the women who met the risen Jesus that he was alive. These were the ones Jesus was about to commission, to charge to preach and teach and baptize, on whom the future of his mission would hang. And here they were, on a mountain in Galilee, ready to see if what the women said was true—that Jesus lived again, and wanted to see them. "When they saw him, they worshiped him; but some doubted." Even when face-to-face with the risen Lord, the light was still weak for some of these disciples, the flames of faith, hope, and love were still flickering, glowing embers almost burned to ash.

But Jesus didn't rebuke them, or cull the doubters from the group. Instead, he commissioned them. He told them what to *do*. And he promised his unending presence. "Remember, I am with you always, to the end of the age."

That's a promise a flickering midlife faith can walk on.

I have laid the bridge. I have freed your wills. Now walk forward.

I have been taking walks for almost a year now, and still am walking, I think, as I'm about to drive home and step forward into a house redolent of chocolate-peppermint cake and glowing with the lights of a season about to begin.

— TRAIL THIRTEEN —

Saying Three Last Words

Abide with me; fast falls the eventide;
the darkness deepens; Lord, with me abide.
When other helpers fail and comforts flee,
Help of the helpless, O abide with me.

–Henry F. Lyte

WALK 38

What Dare We Hope?

"Happy New Year!" We said that in church this morning on the first Sunday of Advent—a form of subtle catechesis, yes, a way of teaching about the rhythms of the liturgical calendar, but more than that, a way of reminding a congregation that our lives as Christians are shaped by days and times and seasons that transcend the secular calendar. But I suspect most people just think it's corny, like singing "Happy Birthday" to the church on Pentecost.

Our church doesn't have pews bolted down, but moveable seats, and this morning they were oriented eastward, in the direction of the rising sun, like the grand cathedrals of Europe. The sun hung low enough in the sky to shine through the east window, and brightness peeked in and through and around the twenty-foot Christmas tree behind the altar. Ginger wore her sunglasses throughout the service, like a movie star hoping to remain incognito.

Our friends Gwen and Joe and their kids lit the first candle of the Advent wreath. Each candle for a Sunday of Advent represents a word, and today's was "hope." As Joe lifted their young son to light the candle, the two of them clicking the lighter several times before it would ignite, their fourth-grade daughter, obviously comfortable in front of people, read a short passage from Isaiah, a few verses about Israel's hope for shalom, for peace, in an undated future:

> . . . they shall beat their swords into plowshares,
> And their spears into pruning hooks;
> nation shall not lift up sword against nation,
> neither shall they learn war any more.
> O house of Jacob,
> come, let us walk in the light of the LORD!

Yes, the light fades, these verses suggest, but there will come a time when the light of love will shine so brightly that all things will be put right. The fire of God's life will burn the dross of anger and hatred and violence from the face of the earth.

And today, it is a promise I yearn for, as I think about the unarmed teenager shot by a police officer in Chicago two days ago; the six children killed in a school bus crash in Chattanooga, Tennessee, five days ago; and the bombings in Aleppo,

Syria, over the past two weeks that killed scores of people. I hope for the shalom the prophet promises, even though I doubt it will come in the way any of us imagine. Will it come from outside of us through one massive divine intervention, one awe-inspiring setting right? Or will it come through the light of Christ burning from within us, burning away the jealousies, hatreds, and fears that fuel the violent tragedies of our world?

If the latter, I want this hope to animate my living and working and writing over the next years. I want it to be the bridge that carries me through my forties and fifties and sixties and beyond—if I'm given a beyond.

And I want it to get me through the next few hours. I *need* it to.

Ginger suggests a family walk, a Christian-New-Year's-Day hike, which is not a bad idea after all the feasting over the past few days; a little exercise can't hurt. And there won't be as many people as on January 1.

We don't get to the nature reserve without a fight, this one over what the children will wear. Its forty-two degrees and cloudless, but this late in the afternoon, the sun will already be setting, so we want the kids to wear toasty winter gear. I set an example by telling them I'm wearing long underwear.

Simeon just wants to go out to eat. Silas, predictably, wants to walk down to the school, where we can throw a Frisbee. And I'm having deja vu.

Mary Clare sits patiently on the couch, a little prophetess of peace, asking if we can *please* not have arguments on this walk because we always seem to argue about something. She's urging us to hammer our verbal swords into ploughshares. So I'm surprised two minutes later when she is the one screaming at me about not having any small gloves that will fit in her pocket if she gets too hot.

"Aren't you the girl who was just sitting there telling me you don't want arguments—and now you are shouting about gloves?" My unhelpful commentary, another verbal sword.

"Are you really wearing long underwear?" Ginger asks.

"I hate being cold."

Simeon runs ahead, his orange jacket complimenting the brown all around. He's mad about an argument in the van I've already forgotten, but when he reaches the pond, he waits on the bench under the bat box for us to catch up. Mary Clare entertains herself by making word-play on "root," as she trips on the ones wrinkling the path.

"We are taking this route—they should rename this path the Root Route. If only we saw a wild pig rooting for food, and had some cheerleaders, rooting us on." She loves this, and so do I.

Before we turn onto Violet, Ginger announces, "I forgot my gloves, and my hands are cold." I'm glad I'm not her father, or I would be compelled to reply in exasperation, "After all that arguing about winter clothes!" I think it instead.

"Is this path hilly?" she asks.

"Really, the whole place is."

She hesitates. "I feel like I'm going to twist my ankle." This has happened before, on a walk at the Mennonite retreat center a month ago, so I offer to let her use my staff, which she declines.

Simeon beats us to the tree-top lookout, his jacket now wrapped around his waist, showing his orange-striped golf shirt. Mary Clare hands me her coat, follows him onto the lookout, says she's not leaving until she finishes cleaning up, then proceeds to "sweep" the leaves off with a stick. As he leaves the tree-top lookout, Simeon grabs my hand without saying a word. He's tired of the wrangling and ready to be close again. We walk and swing arms, and my hand rubs against the coat around his waist, reminding me that I was wrong, at least about the need for winter clothes.

The warmth of a modest, silent reconciliation, with the infusion of hope that passes from Simeon's tender palm into my calloused one—it's enough to get me through to the end of a chilly walk.

Our walk, it occurs to me, is a microcosm of life. There are disagreements and frustrations, open conflicts, hazardous routes, dashes of humor and joy, tender reconciliations. There are mindless mistakes, moments of forgetting, offers of aid. There are infusions of hope that keep us going. There are all of these things, tangled together like a ball of yarn scraps.

Or, if you allow the working of a divine Weaver, not a tangle, but a tapestry—its beauty, its harmony, not always obvious in the moment. And when that tangle or tapestry is your life, a life in its middle, it makes you wonder what we dare hope for. What can we hope for? One answer is what Christians theologians call the eschatological hope—the hope of a great Setting Right.

At one point on the walk Simeon says something annoying to Mary Clare, which I do not hear, but when she comes running to me, angry that Simeon upset her, I unhelpfully suggest, "You need to learn to not let what people say bother you, or you'll be upset for the rest of your life."

Silas, our philosopher, asks, "Even in heaven?"

"Well, maybe not there."

The eschatological hope: that there will be a time when the grace and mercy of God's radiance will rid reality of all of its menacing disruptions and burdensome disfigurements—conflict, war, violence—and the vision of the prophet Isaiah will become a reality. Yes, I hope that the testimony of the saints and the mystics and the prophets and preachers, along with all the sentiments of Advent hymns, come true. I hope that a day is coming when humanity will study war no more, that tears will be wicked from weeping eyes, that death will lose its frightening power.

But the hopes I'm thinking about now are this-side-of-heaven kinds. What can we who are venturing through the threshold called midlife dare to hope? What dare I hope?

Believing that the tangle of yarn won't change, that over the next years the threads of joy, sorrow, conflict, fear, reconciliation might reconfigure, but the realities will stay present, I hope that I can keep learning to say "Yes" to all of it, having been changed by God's own "Yes." I hope that love will flood me before I die, and that in the next decades of life I will find a way to live what I have been learning on these walks.

That death and change are inevitable, but not to be feared.

That God is present in the tangle, if I would but pay attention.

That my vocation is to be myself and to offer that self generously in love.

That I become myself when I practice Mary's *yes* to God.

That I will be truly free when I learn to be at home in the frame of my life.

That the light fades, but never disappears completely.

That I am made for communion—with God, people, and creation.

That my images of God are not God, and neither are my experiences of God; that God is ever challenging my childhood pictures in order to woo me to a mature trust.

That through it all—and into the beyond—there is a Love in, with, by, and under all that is, flashing forth sometimes in unmistakable ways, blazing through like a consuming fire, enveloping us in peace, catalyzing active love like a restless prophet, weaving the threads of my life and our lives—of all creation's being—into a tapestry so elegant and fine we will one day melt in joy to behold it.

A Love that, in the meantime, enlightens our paths with the candle of hope.

WALK 39

Embracing the "P"-Word

After I pray downstairs in the early morning, meditating on the gospel reading for the Second Sunday of Advent—John the Baptist, preparing the way for the Messiah—I go upstairs and dress for a walk. I don't have a coat of camel's hair like John's, though it sounds warm, so I put on two black sweaters, my black coat, brown leather gloves, and my Keble College, Oxford scarf, which makes me look like I've stepped out of a Harry Potter movie; it's thirty-two degrees and I don't like to be cold. I'd rather stay home this morning, but I turn forty-one in less than two weeks, and have two more walks to complete.

As I get out of my car, I hear a woodpecker, and I'm not familiar enough with their calls to identify the kind. But after five minutes of looking, I can't spot it, though I still hear it. Now I think its call is mocking me—a woodpecker-turned-mocking-bird.

The Oak Forest trail, meandering toward Spring Hollow, winds down the side of a hill, back and forth, paralleling the valley toward which it moves, first one direction, then the other. The film of oak leaves shifts, slips under my feet, and I lose my balance, but keep myself from falling with my staff. As I make one turn, I hold on to a small tree with my left had to keep from sliding down the hill.

When I get to Spring Hollow, still upright, thankfully, I see fresh tracks, but since I didn't buy the staff with the track-identification accessory, I'm not sure what animal made them. I'm hoping they don't belong to a cougar or a bear. Thinking about bear tracks reminds me of our trip to the mountains of North Carolina last summer with friends. One morning, I was in my pajamas reading outside, while my family and the family we were visiting were safely inside the cabin watching a black bear skulk up the side of the mountain and into the yard.

"You just left me out there with the bear?" I complained, after I came back inside, ignorant of the threat. I was glad the cabin had a plate-glass window with a wonderful view, since I stayed indoors the rest of the trip.

With visions of bears dancing in my head, I jump when I hear twigs breaking and branches rustling and brush shaking to my right. I fully expect a bear to growl out of the woods and maul me, but what I see instead are deer bounding away, their white tails dancing, flickering like flames—up and down, left and right—until they are gone. They must have thought *I* was a bear.

Usually, even thinking about bears would make me scamper to my car, but today I keep going. I take a longer than usual walk and allow myself to enjoy the thought: *I'm on walk thirty-nine; I'm almost done.* Several times over the last year I've been tempted to give in to the inertia of staying home, and I've been assaulted by self-doubt. *This is a stupid project. No one will publish this, and if it does get published, who will want to read my boring thoughts on nature and midlife?* A few times a new shiny idea emerged, bidding me to drop this midlife project and start something new. *But here I am*, I think. *I'm almost done, almost to the end.* An end, I realize, that will be the beginning of the rest of my life.

I hate the word almost as much as "habit" and "discipline," but if I'm learning anything, it's that I can't avoid it. And I knew I couldn't, when the man in the front row rubbed his bald head and said I was missing something.

A few summers ago, I was giving a lecture on what I called a posture for prayer at a camp in Alabama. While I spoke in a cafeteria transformed into a lecture hall, my handouts spread along the empty salad bar, a skunk could be seen through the floor-to-ceiling windows, nosing around, likely trying to find an entrance into the air-conditioned indoors. Sixty spiritually-hungry souls sat at tables in rows, writing my words feverishly. The bald man wasn't just writing them; he was scrutinizing them.

I was talking about how to be receptive to God in prayer, about the metaphorical posture of prayer that keeps us "open and available to the work of God's Spirit in our lives"—a phrase I uttered no less than ten times; I wanted them to get the point. I had packed everything I'd learned from mystics like John of the Cross, Thomas Kelly, and Thomas Merton into the lecture: be open, be available, allow God to work in you. Prayer, I said, is our open allowing, our being passively available to God's presence. I listed what I took to be qualities of this passive availability. And I supported my assertions with quotations from the saints.

But the bald man in the front row wasn't buying it. He raised his hand, his wiry arm extending high into the air. His other hand rubbed the shadow of whiskers on his shaved head.

"I think you've forgotten one," he said. "Perseverance." He went on to say that he teaches in a community college in Detroit, and many of his students need perseverance more than any other character trait. I had critiqued a do-it-yourself, you-can-have-what-you-want-if-you-just-work-for-it American culture, claiming such a perspective can infect our relationship with God, and here he was saying he sees students who need to practice perseverance most of all. Too many of them drop out, with little to fall back on.

"And shouldn't we be that way with God—shouldn't we keep at it?"

I'd wanted to downplay our effort—maybe because seeing things through to the end had been difficult for me over the years. Perhaps I had avoided talking about perseverance in prayer because I'd been so bad at persevering in other areas of life. I used to have countless journals with only the first few pages of each written in, until I trashed them, tired of them staring at me from the shelves in judgment.

And on these walks, I can't pass an Eagle Scout project bench—Troop 194 must mass-produce these things—without remembering how much I hated scouting, how I never made it past Cub Scouts, and how I hated wearing that blue, scratchy shirt to school every Monday in third grade so I could walk to the scout master's house after school for our meetings. I hated having to earn those badges—whittle safely with a knife, traverse a balance beam, tie a Windsor knot. I hated scout day camp. I'd cry at the front door in the mornings while my ride waited in the street, as I pleaded not to have to go, not to have to swim in the cold pool with the group of boys who were the bad swimmers. "Piranhas," they called us; we never joined the "sharks." I hated canoeing and shooting BB guns. I pressed a used BB through the center of my paper target to make it look like I'd hit the bulls-eye. I hated shooting arrows. I hated sitting under a pavilion making crafts, embossing the leather triangle with outdoorsy images and then weaving a cord through the holes around the edge before adding the beads to the cord to make a tassel. After a couple years, my parents finally let me quit.

I have a gene for starting and not finishing. And here was a seer in the front row, like Nathan in the Old Testament, pointing to David, saying, "You are the man." Here was a man who knew a word I needed, but didn't want to hear: persevere.

Now that I'm finishing this walk, I see that this year has been a lesson in perseverance. And it's a lesson I want to keep learning throughout midlife.

When I was at Keble College, Oxford in my junior year of college, where I bought the red and blue striped scarf I'm wearing, I got very homesick. I couldn't finish. So in early April, with just a month left in the term, I quit. I bought a plane ticket from Heathrow to Cincinnati, went for an Indian feast one last time with my friends, and flew home. Back then, I had a place to go, a home where I belonged, a refuge to which I could flee. Now, in midlife, I *am* home. There is no place else to go. There is no getting out of this, even if I wanted to. There is only perseverance.

There is only showing up, again and again, as authentically as I can. Showing up for Ginger, with an open heart and a generous spirit, as much as I possibly can, for however many more years of this fragile existence we're given. Showing up for the kids, as a dad who is learning love, who makes mistakes, who says "I'm sorry," who's not afraid to cry, and who won't stop showing up even as they grow, change, disappoint, fail, and succeed. Showing up for the work God gives me, the work of teaching and preaching, of getting words on a page that might get into someone's heart and inspire their own perseverance.

And showing up for God, meeting God's own open heart and generous Spirit with one of my own, a heart ever ready to allow that divine generosity and self-giving to remake it in love until I die, and perhaps not stopping even then.

Back at the parking lot, I see the woodpecker. Birdwatchers must also persevere. I see the northern flicker spring from the side of a tree, flap its way above me, the underside of its wings casting a golden glow. When it passes, I see the white spot on its back as it disappears into the trees. Like the deer with their white tails, this bird wears his patch of white brilliantly.

WALK 40

They Call It "Amazing"

I never said it wasn't beautiful. I just don't like being out in it. In Indiana, where I grew up, the roads are straight and flat. Driving in snow was a breeze. And in North Carolina—well, need I say more? But here, there are hills and curves. The kids think I hate it. They complain, "It's just a dusting. We can still see the ground!" And I think, *This is plenty for one year.*

But yesterday evening we received more than a dusting. I left work early and relocated to the library near the house. Reading in the reference room, I looked out the window frequently to watch the snow float down and gauge its accumulation.

When I got home at five, I noticed how our usually debris-strewn yard—red and pink doggy poop bags piled by the front door, waiting for a boy to put them in the trash, pumpkins that have been loitering since Halloween, leaves we've never raked, sticks we haven't gathered—looked fresh, new, beautiful, except for the tracks Mary Clare was making as she trudged up the hill with her sled and sailed back down, over and over, and the ones her brothers had made when they were with her. I discovered the boys inside, sitting on the couch, scarves beside them, hot cups of cocoa cradled in their paws, steam rising in front of their red-cheeked faces, perfectly Norman Rockwell.

Few other humans have been here today, so my feet are writing the first lines on the blank pages of snow. I think of a poem by Billy Collins in which he imagines birds writing stories, poems, and letters with their feet in the snow. The only other writing I can spy, if I'm right, are lyric essays that have been scrawled by deer, who prefer, as I do, to stick to the trails.

The red on the back of a woodpecker's head seems amplified by the white all around, as do the noises I hear: another woodpecker's contact call, the trickle of Harts Run, a nuthatch's gentle honking up and down a tree. A wren shadows me to my right like a Secret Service detail, until it gets spooked and disappears into a hollow stump. When I reach the peak of the Spring Hollow path, I open my notebook to record what I've seen, and the wind exhales suddenly, knocking snow off of a branch and onto my pages. The wind blows again, and snow explodes from limbs all around me and disappears like puffs of smoke.

I never said it wasn't beautiful.

―――――――――――

There are two ways to think about snow, I'm beginning to see. I usually think of it like the snow in Narnia: everlasting as the result of an evil curse. My first thought when winter arrives is, *This will never end*, and I curse the Snow Queen who brings the cursed snow. When I'm in that mood, not even Turkish delight can alter my outlook.

But it occurred to me this morning that there might be another way to view it. I was discussing a sermon by preacher Fred Craddock with students, a sermon about new creation, fresh starts, and forgiveness. "The Bible calls it a new beginning. . . . The Bible calls it a new birth." But Craddock would always rather show you than tell you what he's talking about, rather help you picture it than explain it. So he says,

> The Bible says it's like a snowfall. You get up in the morning early, and you look out: about four inches and there's not a print in it yet. And you look across the valley and what yesterday afternoon was the ugly garbage dumpster is now a mound of glory to God.

When I read that this morning, I thought, *That's what I saw when I got home last night*.
Snow: not an unending curse, but a fresh start.
The Bible also calls it: grace.

―――――――――――

You know when you're standing on the threshold of midlife; you know it when you're there. It can look like an unending winter stretching on and on as far as you can see, no hope of a thaw, no hope of Christmas—a bleak, gray, barren, windy, ice-strewn landscape. And you can want to stay inside as long as possible, drinking hot chocolate on a couch, feet propped on a coffee table.

But it's just possible that grace will strike and wake you up. It's possible that sore feet and tired bones and a failing memory, if you listen to them, will set you on a journey. And along the way someone—a friend, spouse, child, spiritual guide, or, just maybe, a book—will speak a word and help you see the whole thing differently. They'll show you, or you'll find out somehow, if you look hard enough with wide-open eyes and an even wider-open heart, that each moment, each step, each breath— whether you are forty or sixty—is a fresh page, on which to write the discoveries that grace is teaching you, a new moment to live the Love that's still creating you.

Here's something I believe anew with the precarious certainty of faith: *'Tis grace hath brought me safe thus far, and grace will lead me home*.

Questions for Reflection and Discussion

INTRODUCTION

1. As you walk through the years of midlife, what questions arise in you, questions perhaps that drew you to this book?

2. Do you have a sense that these years can be years of discovery?

TRAIL ONE: Facing Death and Change

1. What has it been like for you to grapple with your own mortality?

2. Do you sense God as present in all the changes that accompany midlife, or is God's presence harder for you to detect?

3. How are the changes that you are experiencing in midlife impacting your faith, prayer, and relationships?

TRAIL TWO: Asking, "Who Am I Now?"

1. Are there any attachments that you currently struggle with? Are they inhibiting your ability to see God in your life and in the world?

2. Thomas Merton wrote, "Our vocation is not simply to *be*, but to work together with God in the creation of our own life, our own identity, our own destiny." How do you understand this sentence? How are you cooperating with God in the creation of your identity?

3. What does consenting to God's action in your life—God's making you *you*—look like? How do you understand the idea of consenting to God?

TRAIL THREE: Finding Fruitfulness in the Second Half

1. Do you recognize in yourself a longing to become more fruitful? If so, in what areas of your life? What shape might that fruitfulness take?

2. How do you understand generativity? Are you sensing a desire to be more generative in the second half of your life?

3. How can being generative be a core aspect of your life, not something peripheral, like volunteering?

TRAIL FOUR: Learning to Pay Attention Anew

1. What keeps you from paying careful attention to your life or to God in your life?

2. Can you think of any practices or habits that might help you slow down and savor the life you have right now?

3. Who are the people in your life who help you pay attention to God? How do they help you?

TRAIL FIVE: Confronting Midlife Fears

1. These chapters list many possible midlife fears. What fears are crowding your life?

2. How are you learning to face those fears?

3. What practices or people are helping you to notice the presence of God in the midst of your fears?

TRAIL SIX: Raising Vocational Questions

1. Do you notice any vocational stirrings in your life? What aspects of your vocation might be calling for more attention?

2. Do you understand vocation as an acorn (one thing in you that you have to discover), or is your vocation more like a constellation (many points, some burning more brightly at different times)?

3. As you consider the course of your life, how has your sense of vocation changed? Has your faith impacted your vocation?

TRAIL SEVEN: Hearing the Sounds of Silence

1. How do you experience silence in your life—do you long for it, have too much of it, flee it?

2. Have you ever felt silenced because of doubt or lack of faith? What was that experience like?

3. Have you ever experienced a time when silence helped you find your voice? What was that like?

TRAIL EIGHT: Finding Freedom within a Frame, Part One

1. What aspects of your life in midlife do you feel yourself chafing against?

2. Do you relate to the image of midlife being a time of claustrophobia? If so, how are you dealing with that experience?

3. Do you see any value in the practice of blessing to help you flourish in midlife?

TRAIL NINE: Looking for God

1. Are there images of God that used to be meaningful for you but you find yourself outgrowing? What is that experience like—frightening, freeing?

2. How hard is it for you to imagine that you bear the image of God, that you are a walking theophany?

3. What practices help you to become aware of God both in the world and in your own life?

TRAIL TEN: Finding Freedom within a Frame, Part Two

1. Where are the places in your life where you can experience a sabbath rest, however brief? How badly do you need such rest?

2. How do you grapple with the sense that you are stuck in a rut? Are there any practices you can imagine that could help you appreciate anew the routines of your life?

3. Do you ever experience acedia? When that feeling strikes, how do you confront it?

TRAIL ELEVEN: Heeding the Call of Community

1. Where in your life do you sense a draw toward community?

2. How would you describe the balance between achievement and affiliation in your own life? Which one is most prominent now?

3. How do you understand what it means to be a saint? Do you have a longing for holiness, for transformation?

TRAIL TWELVE: Experiencing God, Following God

1. What has the experience of God in your life been like? How has it changed in midlife?

2. What does it mean to you to call Christ "King"? Are there any images of God you feel yourself increasingly drawn to?

3. What do you do when a vivid religious experience fades? Do you resist the notion of habit in your spiritual life?

TRAIL THIRTEEN: Saying Three Last Words

1. What do you hope for above all else? What's the deepest longing of your heart in these middle years?

2. How do you react to the idea of perseverance as an important virtue both in midlife and in the spiritual life?

3. Grace is one of the most common religious words. What meaning does that word have for you? Do you find hope in the promise of God's gracious presence and guidance?

Author's Notes

First, thank you Ginger for your companionship as I've been on the journey of writing this book, for celebrating the joys of the process with me, listening during the frustrating times, and reading the manuscript before anyone else—laughing at just the right spots. Thank you for your love, constancy, and friendship, which made my writing this possible, as well as so much else. I also want to thank the team at Church Publishing, especially my editor, Milton Brasher-Cunningham, for his meticulous care with this manuscript. My readers should thank him too. If you discovered sentences in this book as meandering as some of the trails I walked, you should have seen them before Milton helped straighten them out. I'm thankful for my dean, Heather Vacek, who supported my proposal to write this book over a sabbatical, even though it doesn't have the footnotes and academic argumentation of a typical professor's book, and for Pittsburgh Theological Seminary's granting me a generous sabbatical to write. Several people read part or all of this manuscript, and I'm grateful for their helpful feedback: Lauren Winner and the others in her "Writing and the Spiritual Life" seminar at the Collegeville Institute, Larry Williams, Craig Kocher, and Jessica Mesman Griffith. My brother, Craig "Bo" Owens, offered invaluable feedback and encouragement, and answered the phone just when I needed to talk. Some of this material was first published, in a slightly different form, in *Rock & Sling*.

I dedicate this book to Simeon, Silas, and Mary Clare. Your tagging along made writing this book so much fun, and I learned more from you than you'll ever know. You bring me such joy.

A note on references: Quotations and allusions to other works are scattered throughout this book. Since it's not academic in nature, I don't feel compelled to burden the reader with lengthy footnotes to prove my scholarly credentials. I hope I have given readers enough information in what follows to track down references should they choose to, and to show that I haven't been making things up.

INTRODUCTION

The Gerald May quotation comes from his *The Dark Night of the Soul* (New York: HarperCollins, 2004), 93. The Frederick Buechner quotation comes from his *Now and Then: A Memoir of Vocation* (New York: HarperCollins, 1983), 31. A discussion of St. Patrick's breastplate can be found in Esther de Waal, *The Celtic Way of Prayer* (New York: Doubleday, 1997), 17–27. I refer to Elizabeth Gilbert's *Eat, Pray, Love* (London: Penguin, 2006) and to Bill Bryson's *A Walk in the Woods* (New York: Broadway, 1998).

TRAIL ONE: Facing Death and Change

Epigraphs come from Madeleine L'Engle, *The Summer of the Great-Grandmother* (San Francisco: HarperCollins, 1988) and Thich Nhat Hanh, *Fear: Essential Wisdom for Getting through the Storm* (New York: HarperCollins, 2012), 53. Ann Hood quotations come from her *Comfort: A Journey Through Grief* (New York: Norton), 119, 87. The quotation from the prayer book comes from *The United Methodist Book of Worship* (Nashville: United Methodist Publishing House, 1992), 155. Denise Levertov's poem "The Avowal" is found in her *The Stream and the Sapphire: Selected Poems on Religious Themes* (New York: New Directions, 1997), 6. Julian of Norwich references come from *Revelations of Divine Love*, trans. Elizabeth Spearing (London: Penguin, 1998), 93 and elsewhere. Quotations from Thich Nhat Hanh are from *Fear*, 52, 30. Jon Sweeney's discussion of Francis is in *When Saint Francis Saved the Church* (Notre Dame, IN: Ave Maria Press, 2014), the quotation about death on page 122. The prayer attributed to Francis can be found in *The Prayers of Saint Francis*, compiled by W. Bader (Hyde Park, NY: New City Press), 93.

TRAIL TWO: Asking, "Who Am I Now?"

Epigraphs come from Thomas Merton, *New Seeds of Contemplation* (New York: New Directions Books, 1961), 204, 31. The references to a well-known prayer by Thomas Merton come from his *Thoughts in Solitude* (New York: Farrar, Straus, Giroux, 1959), 93. References to Virgil's Aeneid come from book IV. The Merton quotation beginning "I wonder if . . ." is from *New Seeds*, 203. The Merton essay, "Things in Their Identity," is in *New Seeds*, 29–46. The Rowan Williams quotation comes from his *Where God Happens: Discovering Christ in One Another* (Boston: New Seeds, 2005), 103. Ronald Rolheiser's discussion of the paschal mystery can be found in his *The Holy Longing: The Search for a Christian Spirituality* (New York: Doubleday, 1999), 141–166. Merton's image of the inner self as a jewel is in *New Seeds*, 38.

TRAIL THREE: Finding Fruitfulness in the Second Half

Epigraph comes from Philip D. Kenneson, *Life on the Vine: Cultivating the Fruit of the Spirit in Christian Community* (Downers Grove, IL: InterVarsity, 1999), 10. The quotation from *Romeo and Juliet* can be found in Act 1, scene 5, lines 53, 54. The quotation from Thomas Kelly comes from *Testament of Devotion* (New York: Harper & Brothers, 1941), 47. The hymn is "Spirit of the Living God" in *The United Methodist Hymnal* (Nashville: The United Methodist Publishing House, 1989), 393. Fred Craddock's reference to the "quiet" Pentecost can be found in his *The Cherry Log Sermons* (Louisville: Westminster John Knox, 2001), 67. Barbara Bradley Hagerty's discussion of generativity and volunteering can be found in her *Life Reimagined: The Science, Art, and Opportunity of Midlife* (New York: Riverhead, 2016), 271–310.

TRAIL FOUR: Learning to Pay Attention Anew

Epigraphs come from David Allen Sibley, *Sibley's Birding Basics* (New York: Alfred A. Knopf, 2002), 5 and Frederick Buechner's *Now and Then, 87.* The Richard Lischer quotation comes from his *Stations of the Heart: Parting with a Son* (New York: Alfred A. Knopf, 2013), 230. The quotation from Helen Macdonald is from her *H Is for Hawk* (New York: Grove Press, 2014), 4. Simone Weil's essay about attention being the substance of prayer is "Reflections on the Right Use of School Studies with a View to the Love of God" in *Waiting for God* (New York: Harper & Row, 1951), 105–116. Hymn 500 is "Spirit of God Descend upon My Heart," by George Croly, in *The United Methodist Hymnal.*

TRAIL FIVE: Confronting Midlife Fears

Epigraphs comes from Pema Chödrön, *When Things Fall Apart: Heart Advice for Difficult Times* (Boston: Shambhala, 2000) and Henri Nouwen, *Spiritual Formation: Following the Movements of the Spirit* (New York: HarperCollins, 2010), 74. Ronald Rolheiser's quotation regarding the symphony of our lives is from his column entitled "Unfinished Symphonies," available on his website, www.ronrolheiser.com. The Samuel H. Miller quotation comes from his *The Life of the Soul* (New York: Harper & Brothers, 1951), 19.

TRAIL SIX: Raising Vocational Questions

Epigraphs come from Barbara Brown Taylor, *The Preaching Life* (Cambridge, MA: Cowley, 1993), 27 and Parker J. Palmer, *Let Your Life Speak* (San Francisco:

Jossey-Bass, 2000), 4. Frederick Buechner's well-known definition of vocation can be found in his *Wishful Thinking: A Theological ABC* (New York: Harper & Row, 1973), 95. Parker Palmer's reflections on discerning vocation by looking at one's childhood can be found in *Let Your Life Speak*, 14–15. Annie Dillard's essay about weasels, "Living Like Weasels," is in *Teaching a Stone to Talk* (New York: Harper-Collins, 1982), 29–34. Kate Hennessy refers to Dorothy Day's fondness for the Dostoyevsky quotation in her *Dorothy Day: The World Will Be Saved by Beauty* (New York: Scribner, 2017), iv.

TRAIL SEVEN: The Sounds of Silence

Epigraphs come from Henri Nouwen, *With Open Hands* (Notre Dame, IN: Ave Maria Press, 1972), 36 and Martin Laird, *Into the Silent Land: A Guide to the Christian Practice of Contemplation* (New York: Oxford, 2006), 2. The description of a rule for an anchoress, including the note that "That life should be lapped about by silence," comes from Andrew Louth's *The Wilderness of God* (Nashville: Abingdon Press, 1991), 71–92. The quotation from Julian of Norwich regarding the indwelling of God in the soul can be found in *Revelations of Divine Love*, 130. Thomas Kelly's reference to "the recreating silences" can be found in *A Testament of Devotion*, 120. James Martin SJ's quotation regarding the examen can be found in his *The Jesuit Guide to (Almost) Everything: A Spirituality for Real Life* (New York: HarperCollins, 2010), 89. The Simone Weil quotation comes from *Waiting for God*, 114.

TRAIL EIGHT: Finding Freedom within a Frame

Epigraphs come from Rowan Williams, *Where God Happens*, 107, and Jonathan Wilson-Hartgrove, *The Wisdom of Stability: Rooting Faith in a Mobile Culture* (Brewster, MA: Paraclete, 2010), 17. The line from Mechthild of Magdeburg is quoted in Sue Monk Kidd, "Live Welcoming to All," *Weavings* vol. XII, no. 5, Sept–Oct, 1997, 8. The Lisa Purpura quotation is from her essay "On Miniatures" in *The Rose Metal Press Field Guide to Flash Nonfiction*, ed. by Dinty W. Moore (Brookline, MA: Rose Metal Press, 2012), 3. Jonathan Rauch's article "The Real Roots of Midlife Crisis" appeared in the December 2014 issue of *The Atlantic*. I found the article on www.theatlantic.com. What I know about Celtic spirituality owes much to Esther de Waal's *The Celtic Way of Prayer*, including the account of Alexander Carmichael's collecting blessings. The blessing for milking a cow is on pages 80–81, and I quote the breastplate of St. Patrick from page 21.

TRAIL NINE: Looking for God

The epigraph is a well-known quotation of Augustine, which I quote from John Paul II's apostolic letter, "Augustinum Hipponensem," August 28, 1986, accessed on the Vatican website, w2.vatican.va. The hymn "This Is My Father's World" is quoted from *The United Methodist Hymnal* (Nashville: The United Methodist Publishing House, 1989), 144. The Denise Levertov poem referenced is "Suspended," found in *The Stream and the Sapphire*, 24. All the quotations from Ignatius of Loyola's "Spiritual Exercises" come from *Ignatius of Loyola: Spiritual Exercises and Selected Works*, ed. by George E. Ganss, S.J. (New York: Paulist Press, 1991). The final meditation, called "Contemplation to Attain Love," is found on 176–177.

TRAIL TEN: Finding Freedom within a Frame, Again

The epigraph comes from Kathleen Norris, *Quotidian Mysteries: Laundry, Liturgy, and "Women's Work"* (New York: Paulist Press 1998), 12. The sermon by Samuel Wells, "A Triangular Faith," was preached at the Duke University Chapel on January 2, 2011. Rev. Wells sent me a manuscript so I could get the quotation right. The *New York Times* reported the benefits of being in nature in a blog post called "How Walking in Nature Changes the Brain," posted July 22, 2015, at well.blogs. nytimes.com. John Cassian's writings on acedia are in *The Philokalia: Volume One*, trans. and ed. by G.E.H. Palmer, Philip Sherrard, and Kallistos Ware (London: Faber and Faber, 1979), 88–91, in which acedia is called "listlessness." The quotation from Kathleen Norris comes from *The Quotidian Mysteries*, 19. The Merton quotation is from his *New Seeds*, 16–17. Barbara Bradley Hagerty discusses humanity's wiring for novelty in *Life Reimagined*, 156–157, and recounts the story of her RV journey in Chapter 6, "The Desert or Oasis of Midlife Marriage." The story of Anthony is found in *The Sayings of the Desert Fathers: The Alphabetical Collection*, trans. Benedicta Ward, SLG (Kalamazoo, MI: Cistercian Publications, 1975), 1–2. The prayer by Ignatius that begins "Give me nothing . . ." is a version I know from memory, but don't know where I learned it. Another version can be found in *Ignatius of Loyola*, 177.

TRAIL ELEVEN: Heeding the Call of Community

Epigraphs come from Dietrich Bonhoeffer, *Dietrich Bonhoeffer Works, Volume 5: Life Together* and *Prayerbook of the Bible*, trans. by Daniel Bloesch and James Burtness, ed. by Geffrey Kelly (Minneapolis: Fortress, 1996), 38 and Henri Nouwen, *Making All Things New: An Invitation to the Spiritual Life* (New York: HarperCollins, 1981), 82. The quotation from Henri Nouwen comes from *Spiritual Direction:*

Wisdom for the Long Walk of Faith (New York: HarperCollins, 2006), 115. The Einstein quotation I remember hearing being attributed to him, but don't remember where. The Richard Rohr quotation comes from *Falling Upward: A Spirituality for the Two Halves of Life* (San Francisco: Jossey-Bass, 2011), 4. The account of Merton's mystical experience is quoted in Jim Forest, *Living with Wisdom: A Life of Thomas Merton*, Revised Edition (Maryknoll, NY: Orbis, 2008), 133–134. The *New York Times* reported on the difficulty of midlife friendship in an article by Alex Williams called "Why Is It Hard to Make Friends Over 30?" on July 13, 2012. I found the article on www.nytimes.com. Dwight Judy discusses achievement and affiliation in his *Discerning Life Transitions: Listening Together in Spiritual Direction* (New York: Morehouse, 2010), 69–72. The story about Francis, "Brother Robber," is writing by Helene Christaller and can be found in *Home for Christmas: Stories for Young and Old*, compiled by Miriam LeBlanc (Farmington, PA: Plough Publishing, 2002), 1–7. The Bonhoeffer quotation regarding the length of Scripture is in *Dietrich Bonhoeffer Works: Volume 5*, 61. The Louis Savary quotation is from his *The New Spiritual Exercises: In the Spirit of Pierre Teilhard de Chardin* (New York: Paulist, 2010), 45.

TRAIL TWELVE: Experiencing God, Following God

The epigraph comes from Kelly, *A Testament of Devotion*, 31. Other references to Kelly are either from this book as well, or from the Thomas R. Kelly Papers at Haverford College. The quotation from Merton is from his *New Seeds*, 205. The Rowan Williams quotation comes from his *On Christian Theology* (Oxford: Blackwell, 2000), 77.

TRAIL THIRTEEN: Saying Three Last Words

The epigraph comes from the hymn "Abide with Me," by Henry F. Lyte, in *The United Methodist Hymnal*, 700. The Billy Collins poem referred to is "Ornithography" in his *Ballistics* (New York: Random House, 2008), 83–84. The Fred Craddock sermon is "Have You Ever Heard John Preach," in *A Chorus of Witnesses: Model Sermons for Today's Preacher*, ed. Thomas G. Long and Cornelius Plantinga Jr. (Grand Rapids, MI: Eerdmans), 35–43. "Amazing Grace," by John Newton, is in *The United Methodist Hymnal*, 377.